T0316688

Cambridge Elements

Elements in Organization Theory
edited by
Nelson Phillips
Imperial College London
Royston Greenwood
University of Alberta

STAKEHOLDER THEORY

Concepts and Strategies

R. Edward Freeman
University of Virginia

Jeffrey S. Harrison
University of Richmond

Stelios Zyglidopoulos
Kedge Business School

CAMBRIDGE
UNIVERSITY PRESS

CAMBRIDGE
UNIVERSITY PRESS

University Printing House, Cambridge CB2 8BS, United Kingdom

One Liberty Plaza, 20th Floor, New York, NY 10006, USA

477 Williamstown Road, Port Melbourne, VIC 3207, Australia

314–321, 3rd Floor, Plot 3, Splendor Forum, Jasola District Centre,
New Delhi – 110025, India

79 Anson Road, #06–04/06, Singapore 079906

Cambridge University Press is part of the University of Cambridge.

It furthers the University's mission by disseminating knowledge in the pursuit of
education, learning, and research at the highest international levels of excellence.

www.cambridge.org
Information on this title: www.cambridge.org/9781108439282
DOI: 10.1017/9781108539500

First published 2018

A catalogue record for this publication is available from the British Library.

ISBN 978-1-108-43928-2 Paperback
ISSN 2397-947X (online)
ISSN 2514-3859 (print)

Stakeholder Theory

Concepts and Strategies

DOI: 10.1017/9781108539500
First published online: August 2018

R. Edward Freeman
University of Virginia

Jeffrey S. Harrison
University of Richmond

Stelios Zyglidopoulos
Kedge Business School

Abstract: The stakeholder perspective is an alternative way of understanding how companies and people create value and trade with each other. Freeman, Harrison, and Zyglidopoulos discuss the foundation concepts and implementation of stakeholder management as well the advantages this approach provides to firms and their managers. They present a number of tools that managers can use to implement stakeholder thinking, better understand stakeholders, and create value with and for them. The Element concludes by discussing how managers can create stakeholder-oriented control systems and by examining some of the important stakeholder-related issues that are worthy of future scholarly and managerial attention.

Keywords: enterprise strategy, stakeholder control systems, stakeholder management, stakeholder theory, value creation

ISBNs: 9781108439282 (PB), 9781108539500(OC)
ISSNs: 2397-947X (online), 2514-3859 (print)

Contents

1 The Origin and Foundation of Stakeholder Management

Some people were shocked to hear of a systemic problem in the venerable Wells Fargo Bank, where employees had been creating new credit accounts for their customers without their knowledge. Other people were not particularly surprised. After all, Volkswagen was caught programming its diesel engines to fool emissions testing equipment and Enron's off-book financial deals led to bankruptcy and financial disaster for thousands of employees and investors. In addition, Johns-Manville knew that producing asbestos was harming its employees, yet the company concealed this information instead of addressing the problem. So the Wells Fargo incident, though disappointing, is just one example of a larger problem in business today. At the core of these sorts of problems is an organizational value system, supported by an incentive system, that puts short-term financial profits ahead of the welfare of one or a group of stakeholders (Stout, 2012).

Stakeholders are groups and individuals that have a valid interest in the activities and outcomes of a firm and on whom the firm relies to achieve its objectives (Freeman, 1984; Freeman et al., 2007a). For most business firms, which are the focus of this Element, primary stakeholders include customers, employees, suppliers of tangible goods and services, suppliers of capital (including shareholders if the firm is a corporation or similar form), and the communities in which the firm operates. Other common stakeholders vary in importance depending on the nature of the firm and its industry. They often include government officials and regulators (in addition to those at the community level), special-interest groups, consumer advocate groups, nongovernmental organizations (NGOs), the media, unions, and competitors. These additional stakeholders are sometimes called secondary because they do not contribute as directly to the value-creating processes of the firm (Freeman et al., 2007a; Phillips, 2003). We do not mean to imply that they are not important, but rather that, from a practical perspective, much of a manager's time and attention will (and should) focus on the stakeholders who contribute most to the value the firm creates – the primary stakeholders.

1.1 Origin of the Stakeholder Perspective

The stakeholder perspective came into being as an alternative way of understanding how companies and people create value and trade with each other in a world where there is very little stability and certainty (Freeman et al., 2010). It was designed to solve three interconnected problems. First, how can we create value in a turbulent world? Second, how are we to understand the ethics of capitalism? Third, what should we be teaching in business schools?

The stakeholder perspective has often been seen as a competing perspective to the shareholder value maximization perspective that has dominated business thinking for more than half a century (Stout, 2012). This is somewhat misleading, however, as stakeholder theory acknowledges the importance of shareholders and shareholder value, although it also argues that shareholders aren't the only group that is important to running a successful business. Shareholder value maximization promotes the perspective that the primary responsibility of top managers is to maximize profits so that shareholders receive the largest returns possible. Stakeholder theory suggests that the world is far more complex and that successful business firms create value (only some of which is financial) for all key stakeholders (Freeman et al., 2010).

The shareholder perspective led to a great deal of short-term thinking in organizations, often at the expense of longer-term organizational health. An obsession with bottom-line profitability helped stimulate the sort of behavior we described in the first paragraph. However, around the same time that shareholder primacy was gaining prominence, a few others were discussing a very different management approach. The stakeholder perspective, as we understand it today, was first delineated in a comprehensive fashion in a book titled *Strategic Management: A Stakeholder Approach* (Freeman, 1984). It was written as a practical guide for managers and students of strategic management, and much of what we will share in this Element has its roots in that book.

The strategic management discipline did not immediately absorb the stakeholder approach into its mainstream, although it was the subject of much debate and development elsewhere, predominantly in the business ethics discipline. However, over the decades since the mid-1980s, the stakeholder perspective has gained significant traction in strategic management as well as in numerous other fields, including public administration, law, marketing, operations, healthcare, accounting, and finance (Freeman et al., 2010). We attribute this rise in importance to its practicality in dealing with a business world that is increasing in complexity and turbulence, and to society's increasing sensitivity to the ethical (or unethical) behavior of organizations (Freeman et al., 2007a).

1.2 Core Concepts of Stakeholder Management

Although this Element takes a practical approach, we would first like to establish a foundation of understanding upon which we will build the concepts and techniques found in later sections. We will base our approach to stakeholder management on the following seven core concepts (Freeman et al., 2007a, 2010).

Concept 1: A Managerial Focus

The stakeholder perspective is useful in that it describes what managers actually do. Business executives manage stakeholders (Freeman, 1984), and the manner in which those stakeholders are managed influences the value a business firm creates (or destroys). The real challenge is to determine best practices in managing stakeholders, and to determine the contexts in which those practices are most likely to lead to the best value-creating results. "Management" here does not mean manipulation and exploitation, but how to craft relationships in which all of a firm's key stakeholders win over time, or what might be called "win–win–win–win–win" relationships. To a great extent, that is what this Element is about. Based on our experiences as scholars and consultants who have developed and applied stakeholder theory in many types of organizations for the past several decades, we intend to share with you some of the ideas and tools we have found most useful in managing stakeholders.

Concept 2: A Moral Foundation

Stakeholder management is based on a moral foundation that includes respect for humans and their basic rights, integrity, fairness, honesty, loyalty, freedom to choose, and assumption of responsibility for the consequences of the actions a firm takes (Freeman et al., 2010; Phillips, 2003). The fact that stakeholder management is a moral approach is inherently satisfying to those managers who practice it. Their consciences tend to be less encumbered with feelings of guilt, they need not "fake" virtue around colleagues and stakeholders, they have a moral code that helps them make decisions, and they can enjoy a greater sense of self-worth. This is not to say that they do not make mistakes, but they have a set of guidelines that are somewhat universally understood and tend to be respected by those around them. They don't have to spend a great deal of energy rationalizing their decisions.

Concept 3: An Overarching Purpose (Enterprise Strategy)

The purpose of a firm can be defined in terms of what it does for its stakeholders, which is a part of what might be called a firm's enterprise strategy (Freeman and Gilbert, 1988). Firms should ask why they are doing the things they are doing. What is their purpose? What do they stand for? The answers tend to lead to a statement of purpose and values. They both empower and proscribe action.

What does the firm value? Perhaps the best way to determine the real values in a firm is to trace decisions back to the individuals who made them and their motivations for these decisions (Pastin, 1986). For example, a manager may allow an employee to arrive late to work without penalty to be able to attend an award ceremony for a child, or the manager may require the employee to miss the award ceremony to show loyalty to the firm. Either of these decisions is likely a result of a value that is held by the manager and reinforced by the firm through past decisions made by the manager or others in the firm, and possibly even communicated through a corporate values statement or an address or memo from a top manager. Similarly, an employee may accept a returned product from a customer even if the product is damaged, or may turn the customer away unsatisfied. These sorts of decisions tend not to be made in isolation of other decisions. Decisions within firms form a pattern, and the pattern reveals the true values of the firm.

Another term that is sometimes used to describe this aspect of a firm's enterprise strategy is stakeholder culture (Jones et al., 2007). Firms form what might be called a predominant stakeholder culture that provides guidance in how managers and employees should treat stakeholders. There is wide variance in stakeholder cultures across organizations. Stakeholder culture represents an opportunity for a firm to differentiate itself from competitors and other firms. That is, especially in a world in which corporate scandals and poor stakeholder treatment are common, firms that adopt a stakeholder-based culture as a part of their enterprise strategy have an opportunity to distinguish themselves in the eyes of both current and potential stakeholders. We will explore this important concept further in later sections.

Finally, enterprise strategy also deals with a firm's responsibility to society (Freeman et al., 2007a). Capitalism is allowed to function only because society allows it to function. The modern corporation (and similar forms of organization) is under attack because of manifest corruption and greed, harm to the environment, harm to stakeholders, and a perceived attitude of irresponsibility with regard to some of the actions corporations take. The sustainability movement grew out of societal forces more than corporate initiatives (Harrison and van der Laan Smith, 2015). Also, new regulations tend to come from corporate inattention to things that are important to society. Consequently, firms should take the initiative and determine for themselves, and in advance of new regulations, boycotts, or bad press, what their responsibilities are to society.

At the heart of enterprise strategy is what might be called the "ethical leader" (Freeman et al., 2007a). The chief executive officer (CEO) and other top managers set the tone for a firm's values, and its responsibilities to stakeholders and the broader society in which the firm operates. Ethical leaders use tools such as example, internal and external communications, and rewards systems to both establish and reinforce a firm's enterprise strategy.

Concept 4: Creation of Both Economic and Noneconomic Value

The value a business firm creates for its stakeholders is more than economic in nature, and can include a wide variety of other benefits associated with human factors such as personal development, affiliation, freedom to choose, esteem, and happiness (Harrison and Wicks, 2013). These benefits tend to be considered when firms discuss employees, but they extend also to other stakeholders. For example, customers, suppliers, community members, and even financiers can enjoy feelings of pride through affiliation with a firm they consider virtuous, as well as happiness if they are treated well.

This particular concept is important to the stakeholder approach to management because these noneconomic factors have to be included in discussions of stakeholder welfare. Stakeholders look at the whole package of what they get from a firm when they decide whether to engage and/or continue to engage with it (Harrison et al., 2010). They tend to weigh the total "utility" (or value) they get from interactions against what they would get from interactions with a different firm (Harrison and Wicks, 2013). These are sometimes called opportunity costs, and even though there may be costs associated with switching to another firm (switching costs), at some point stakeholders will do so if they believe their opportunity costs are too high. Consider an employee who realizes she is being underpaid and, to make matters worse, does not feel respected by managers in the firm. At some point the employee's perception that she would be treated better at another firm, and possibly even paid more, will move her from her comfort zone, and she will seek employment elsewhere. With regard to suppliers, we are aware of a firm that walked away from a very big contract with Walmart, America's largest retailer, because the CEO felt that he was being mistreated. The same logic applies, in both positive and negative ways, to other stakeholders.

In a sense, all stakeholders hold "customer-like" power in that, in a society that allows freedom of choice, they can decide whom to trade with. They may have resources the firm needs, such as money, talent, time, knowledge, or physical goods, and they can choose to engage with the firm that they believe will provide them with the package of utility that is most to their liking, and often noneconomic factors are a big part of their decision-making processes. Consider, for example, a consumer who buys meat exclusively at Whole Foods because Whole Foods has a value system that prevents cruelty to animals. Also, many employees continue to work for an employer in spite of low pay because of the happiness they experience from affiliation with a company that has an attractive moral code. However, it is important not to reduce stakeholder relationships to a set of individual transactions. As trust develops with stakeholders, a presumption develops that the relationship will continue over time (Freeman, 1984). Shared understanding and mutual interconnected interests begin to trump any formal contracts that are produced at the beginning of a relationship (Bridoux and Stoelhorst, 2016; Jones et al., 2018). This discussion leads naturally to the next core concept – reciprocity.

Concept 5: Reciprocity

Humans respond positively when they are treated well and negatively when they are treated poorly. Reciprocity means that it is possible for a firm to gain net economic benefits from additional investments of time, money, and resources in serving stakeholders, in spite of the incremental costs of such investments (Bosse et al., 2009). As with the previous concept, much of reciprocity has to do with perceived opportunity costs. So an employee who believes she or he is being provided with more value through working with one firm rather than another (including value provided from salary, benefits, respect, inclusion, affiliation, perquisites, and so forth) will tend to give back more to the company in terms of effort, commitment, sharing of important information, enthusiasm, and loyalty. Similarly, consider a customer who believes she or he is getting a better deal in terms of the value received for the price paid, respect, feelings of affiliation with a virtuous organization, and the quality of service provided. This sort of customer will tend to be more enthusiastic about the product and the company, will share this enthusiasm with others, and will buy from the company again when the opportunity arises.

Some companies make a deliberate effort to give back to their communities through a variety of means such as providing employees for local service efforts or contributing to local charities. They can also enjoy benefits from reciprocity. Members of communities in which these sorts of companies operate will want to work for the company. Its leaders will be more likely to approve building permits for expansion or extend tax breaks or other incentives for doing so, and to approve or encourage infrastructure investments that are helpful to the firm. Stakeholders who are treated very well become "fans" of the firm rather than simply suppliers, customers, or employees.

We have highlighted employees, customers, and communities here, but the same sort of reciprocity exists for all of a firm's primary stakeholders and, to some extent, for secondary stakeholders as well. These secondary effects are explainable, in part, through the advantage of a good reputation.

Concept 6: Reputation

A business firm gains a reputation (Fombrun, 1996) from the way it treats its stakeholders, and this reputation can influence how attractive the firm is to both existing and potential future stakeholders (Freeman et al., 2007a; Harrison et al., 2010; Jones et al., 2018). For example, a potential customer can become aware of how a firm treats its customers through word-of-mouth or through consumer reports and media coverage. Potential employees tend to find a stakeholder-oriented company a much more attractive prospect relative to other companies that do not have such a reputation. Suppliers, communities, and financiers likewise respond favorably to a firm with a good reputation and unfavorably to one with a tainted reputation (Fombrun and Shanley, 1990).

An important secondary effect is also evident from the strength of a firm's reputation. Secondary stakeholders such as the media and special-interest groups may not have direct interactions with a firm; however, they become aware of the way a firm treats its stakeholders. This awareness can lead these stakeholders to engage in negative reporting, lobbying for new regulations, organization of boycotts, or other behaviors that can reduce the amount of value the firm produces. A strong positive reputation makes these sorts of behaviors less likely.

Concept 7: Stakeholder Interests Converge Over Time

An important part of the stakeholder discussion is whether the interests of one stakeholder must be traded off against the interests of another stakeholder (Freeman, 1984; Freeman et al., 2010). In other words, does increasing the amount of value provided to one stakeholder reduce the amount of value available to one or more other stakeholders? We would like to share three points on this important question.

First, an increase in value to one stakeholder does not have to be accompanied by a decrease in value to another one because the amount of value a firm creates is not fixed. Think of slices of a pie, with each stakeholder getting an even slice. If the pie were fixed in size, then the only way one stakeholder could get a bigger slice is if another one gets a smaller slice. But the real synergy occurs as an increased allocation of value to one or more stakeholder results in a successful business outcome, as well as reciprocal behavior, and thus the creation of even more value by the firm. The pie gets larger, which means that each slice can expand. One of the criticisms of the larger pie concept is that it takes time for reciprocity to result in incremental value, and so some stakeholders will lose in the short term. This may be true in some cases, but not all. An astute decision maker can often find mutually beneficial solutions that lead to increased value for some stakeholders with little or no loss of value to other stakeholders.

Of course, over time avoiding trade-offs is even easier to do, and this is our second point. If a particular stakeholder has been treated very well in the past, he or she is much more likely to be accepting of a firm's decision that would seem to take value from him or her in the short term. This is because stakeholders have memories, and so what may seem like an unattractive trade-off in the here and now may not look unattractive if it is considered part of a series of decisions the firm has made over a period of years. Alternatively, if value is allocated to one stakeholder over another in the short term, and the firm communicates the future value such a decision will create, the losing stakeholder can anticipate that the immediate loss of value will be compensated for when that additional value is created. This sort of thinking is going to work only for a firm that has a well-established record of being fair with stakeholders – a firm with a stakeholder-oriented enterprise strategy.

Third, a stakeholder-oriented manager will attempt to make decisions that are beneficial to one or more stakeholders without hurting the others (win–win–win–win–win decisions). Some decisions make this an easy objective to accomplish. For example, the decision to launch a new product can have positive effects for employees, suppliers, financiers, and even communities. This is a mutually beneficial decision. Sometimes, though, tough decisions have to be made, such as closing a plant that has been losing money for years. The first stakeholder who comes to mind in this situation is probably the employee; however, firms have developed a number of mechanisms to soften the blow or even enhance the situation for employees, including generous severance packages, outplacement programs, and transfers to new locations of an employee's choosing (complete with moving expenses). There will always be employees who are not satisfied regardless of what is done for them, but the typical employee would see these sorts of actions as positive, and possibly even attractive, especially compared with simply being let go.

These actions cost money, so don't they hurt shareholders? Actually, if the plant was losing money, closing it is likely to boost the share price of the firm, regardless of severance and relocation costs, so the shareholder will be better off. Suppliers and communities are a little tougher to satisfy in such circumstances, but loyalty to suppliers in terms of using them at other plant locations can go a long way toward helping them to feel well treated. A firm's actions to reduce the impact on the community it is leaving are going to vary depending on each unique situation, but donating the land upon which the operation was located for creation of a park or donating the building to a college might be possibilities. Also, remember that most managerial decisions, even major ones, are not as difficult as this one in terms of being fair to stakeholders or making them feel well treated. The concept here is that managers should attempt to look for solutions that minimize or eliminate losses of value to each of their stakeholders.

1.3 Organization of Sections

We have organized the sections in the Element around questions managers have regarding how to manage stakeholders. Section 2 is about why a stakeholder approach is necessary for twenty-first-century businesses. Section 3 addresses the tricky problem of who is a stakeholder. In Section 4 we explain how the stakeholder value creation process works. Sections 5 through 7 address particular tools to implement stakeholder thinking. These tools have been developed over a number of years and many executives have found them quite useful. Section 5 develops some analytical tools for understanding stakeholders and their behavior. Section 6 provides some strategy development tools for creating value with and for stakeholders. Section 7 focuses on stakeholder-oriented control systems. Finally, in Section 8 we examine some of the important stakeholder-related issues that are worthy of significant scholarly and managerial attention in the future and offer a set of further readings.

2 Why a Stakeholder Approach?

Steve Jobs, the legendary late CEO of Apple, was once asked in an interview what his longer-term strategy was. He replied, "I am going to wait for the next big thing" (Rumelt, 2011: 14). Such an opportunity appeared in the music business and Jobs took full advantage of it with iTunes® and the iPod®. At the turn of the twentieth century, the music industry was suffering from the incursion of digital technology. Digital technology allowed for the free downloading of song tracks without paying music companies or artists their usual fees. However, it seemed that most consumers, who in principle benefited from being able to download the music, did not really want to do it illegally, but felt they had no legal alternative. So, Jobs created a legal alternative that allowed everybody to win – the music companies, the artists, Apple, and the consumer, who enjoyed better service and did not have to steal (Isaacson, 2011). In short, Jobs managed to weave together the interests of multiple stakeholders through a winning strategy for everybody, including his company.

This example illustrates some of the benefits that a broad stakeholder perspective can provide to business firms and their stakeholders. These benefits are even more pronounced in dynamic industries in which the interests of stakeholders are highly interconnected. In this section, in addressing the question "why a stakeholder approach?" we argue that stakeholder-oriented management enables managers to better perform four crucial and highly interconnected activities: (1) creating value – especially in dynamic markets, (2) innovating, (3) dealing with the inclusivity and interconnectedness of various relevant groups and individuals, and (4) better addressing ethical issues. These activities are important not only for the long-term survival and success of business firms, but also for the contributions they make to society.

2.1 Value Creation

The first function of business firms, one could argue, is the creation of value for stakeholders and, from a broader perspective, for society as a whole. To do so, firms need plentiful resources that are controlled by various stakeholders, each with their own motivations and goals. This aspect of stakeholder management has been extensively discussed in the literature, often with the idea that firms have to trade off the needs of one stakeholder against another. However, by focusing on stakeholder trade-offs, managers miss out on some of the most important contributions that stakeholders can make to the value creation process (Freeman et al., 2007a). In addition to the various tangible resources that stakeholders control and are needed by the firm, stakeholders also have valuable information, expertise, and insights that can help a firm design better value creation strategies, in addition to understanding where the major sources of value are going to come from in the future (Harrison et al., 2010).

To create value, firms need to see the world through the eyes of their multiple stakeholders and be able to harness not only the resources their stakeholders control, but also the information and insights that these stakeholders can provide. These insights and information will enable firms to find new ways of creating value and grow the value pie for all to share. In a sense, one could say that an important aspect of the stakeholder approach is its emphasis on this empathy that allows firms close contact with their stakeholders, and enables them to harness their insights, know-how, and information, which helps them avoid getting trapped into a "this is the way we have always done it" mindset.

It is not only the current creation of value that matters. Because industries are dynamic, firms must be able to anticipate *where* new value is going to be created in the future. In 1981, when IBM introduced its first personal computer (PC), it focused on its main competitor in the microcomputer market, Apple. For more than a decade, IBM did very well against Apple. The IBM PC became the industry standard and Apple was almost driven out of business. However, though IBM's strategy worked at first, the company failed to understand where the real value in the computer industry was going to be in the future – the operating system and the chip inside. As a result, Microsoft and Intel dominated these most valuable (in the 1990s) segments of the PC industry, while IBM was left competing in the commodity (hardware) part of the industry. Eventually IBM left the PC industry completely.

A close relationship with stakeholders encourages the transfer of vital information from them, which allows a firm to better predict important trends and establish value-creating strategies that take advantage of them. We will provide more on the mechanics of how this happens in Section 3.

2.2 Innovation

Within this "broader" value creation domain, innovation is one of the most important issues. In using the term innovation, we are referring to new products and services as well as new organizational and technological processes used in their creation and delivery (Dougherty, 1992; Utterback and Abernathy, 1975). Both kinds of innovation can benefit from a stakeholder approach because in both cases it is the harnessing of the knowledge embedded in various stakeholders that makes the difference between success and failure. Viewing innovation through a multiple-stakeholder perspective allows firms to more broadly identify the most relevant internal or external stakeholders; be more inclusive of their interests; draw on their knowledge and expertise; and gain acceptance from them when the new product, service, or process is introduced.

Regarding new product and service development, it is well established that success depends to a great degree on the information provided by customers (Calantone and Di Benedetto, 1988; Walter, 2003). However, a stakeholder approach can help firms gather information and gain acceptance from all relevant stakeholders (Driessen et al., 2013). Suppliers and employees, and in some cases financiers, regulators, or communities, are part of a team effort to create new products and services. Regular interactions with stakeholders from the earliest stages of product or service development enable firms to avoid unpleasant surprises later on and to design open interaction patterns and develop common language about their new products or services before launch. Basically, integration of information from all relevant stakeholders allows firms to develop better products and services with higher probabilities of being accepted. The importance of including a diverse set of stakeholders becomes even more evident in technologically advanced industries such as medical devices, where new products rely on information from and cooperation with physicians, hospital administrators, patients, and insurance companies, just to mention a few of the many relevant stakeholders (Harrison and Thompson, 2014). Sections 5, 6, and 7 provide tools to help firms develop capabilities related to gathering and using information from stakeholders.

In addition to product and service development, a stakeholder approach can also contribute to process innovation. Research suggests that two major issues can become obstacles in the implementation of new processes within firms (Birkinshaw and Mol, 2006). They are the degree to which various stakeholders accept or do not accept the required changes and the unexpected interactions of these changes between different systems. Similar to product and service development, inclusion of all relevant stakeholders can help with the acceptance issue for process innovations. After all, many stakeholders have the ability to block or diminish the effectiveness of a new process. However, early and frequent interactions with relevant stakeholders are also quite important in identifying unexpected systems interactions. Stakeholders tend to have first-hand knowledge that can help a firm identify these previously unexpected interactions between various production and information systems, interactions that the firm's managers might have missed if they considered only formally documented interrelationships. Stakeholders know much about the less formal relationships, but this information has to be tapped.

2.3 Inclusivity and Interconnectedness

Even if it has become a cliché to say so, it is nevertheless true that modern firms operate in a global environment where they face an increasing number of diverse and often interdependent stakeholders. Within such an environment, a stakeholder approach enables firms to be more inclusive not only in identifying relevant stakeholders and their interests, but also in developing the capability necessary to deal with such multiple and diverse stakeholders. Such a capability can be seen as both preventing firms from making strategic mistakes and as a source of advantage in competing with other firms.

For example, when Shell UK tried to decommission its Brent Spar platform in the North Sea by sinking it into the Atlantic Ocean, it faced boycotts from its European consumers (led by Greenpeace) and endured much negative publicity that damaged its reputation (Zyglidopoulos, 2002). In the end, Shell had to reverse its decision and dispose of the Brent Spar platform on land. The miscalculation that led Shell UK into this extremely costly controversy was the fact that the firm did not include in its initial planning phases how its European stakeholders felt about this proposal, nor did they adequately account for the influence Greenpeace had on these stakeholders. Learning from this crisis, Shell engaged in a major restructuring of its External Affairs division to develop its capability to deal with various stakeholders and issues that could impact the corporation and its objectives. This sort of capability allows firms to deal effectively with various stakeholders, and can lead to a competitive advantage for firms over the long run (Barnett, 2007).

Broader inclusion of multiple stakeholders allows firms to avoid some of the problems associated with the shareholder primacy approach mentioned in Section 1. A major problem with shareholder primacy is that managers tend to focus on the conflict between shareholders and other stakeholders rather than finding ways to create value for all involved (Freeman et al., 2010). Those who favor shareholder primacy often argue that stakeholder theory justifies managers allocating resources to unproductive uses, defined as uses that do not contribute directly to or may even reduce firm profitability. For example, they might argue that giving back to the community through volunteer programs or providing highly attractive benefits to employees wastes resources and reduces returns to shareholders (Jensen, 1989). As such, it might even be considered irresponsible. However, it has become apparent that shareholder primacy itself can encourage irresponsible behavior (e.g., Enron). In contrast, a stakeholder approach encourages greater moral accountability (Phillips et al., 2003). It helps resolve the conflict between stakeholders and shareholders by focusing on strategies that create value for everyone, including shareholders. These value-creating strategies are inclusive rather than focusing on one or a small set of stakeholders, and therefore also help a firm deal better with existing and potential interconnections among stakeholders.

2.4 The Inseparability of Business and Ethics

All major business decisions have a moral/ethical component to them (Freeman, 1994). Sometimes we have challenged groups of managers or students to think of even one business decision that has no ethical component. They often revert to what they think are merely financial decisions such as the decision to increase dividends. We then ask them questions like, "If a firm increases dividends, where will the money come from? To what extent does such a decision favor a shareholder who provided capital at some point vs. an employee who works 40–50 hours every week to create value for the firm and is worthy of a raise?" It doesn't take many questions before our participants realize that it is impossible to separate the instrumental (or practical) components of a managerial decision from the normative (or moral/ethical).

Nevertheless, some managers still believe that some managerial decisions are strictly about business, and any ethical considerations are secondary, or simply not important at all. This perspective, called the "separation thesis" or "separation fallacy," can have negative consequences with respect to the contributions of businesses within society (Freeman, 1994). For example, business decisions made in the absence of ethical considerations provide opportunities for immoral managerial behavior under the excuse that "this is only business" or "this is how it is always done."

Also, the separation fallacy can lead companies to address ethical concerns only as an afterthought, as in cases in which firms engage in corporate social responsibility programs in an effort to make up for the harm they do. One might question whether a firm that engages in socially undesirable or even harmful activities suddenly becomes a good corporate citizen because it donates clean water to flood victims, provides food for homeless people, or builds a park in an urban neighborhood. Such a firm may have even published a code of ethics or a statement of values, but its behavior is contradictory, and stakeholders eventually tend to figure out that this firm is not authentic (Cording et al., 2014), resulting in a damaged reputation and negative reciprocity from stakeholders (Bosse et al., 2009).

Given such negative consequences deriving from the acceptance of the separation fallacy, one of the major contributions of stakeholder theory is that it rejects it, and at the very least avoids such consequences. The best way to appear authentic is to be authentic. A firm that manages for its stakeholders doesn't just dress up its reputation with a values statement or code of ethics; it lives by these guidelines. Rejection of the separation fallacy also allows managers to consider more of the full impact the firm's actions have on stakeholders, and thus to design and implement strategies that have fewer potential pitfalls and are more sustainable over the long run. Also, a stakeholder approach allows managers to have a more comprehensive and inclusive view of their firm's overall obligations in society (Freeman et al., 2010). It provides a strong answer to the criticism that capitalism is corrupt and rigged to benefit the rich at the expense of the poor. It helps address opposition movements such as Occupy Wall Street.

In this section, we answered the question, "why a stakeholder approach?" We addressed this question by assuming a teleological position and identifying the benefits that follow from the adoption of a stakeholder approach. These benefits fall into two general categories: long-term value creation and avoidance of unethical behavior that can hinder the sustainability of the firm's mission. In short then, the answer to the question "why a stakeholder approach?" is "because it works better for all."

3 Who Is a Stakeholder?

Typically an executive's most limited resource is time. How much time should be spent in planning, communicating, meeting with people, organizing or attending events, and collecting or analyzing information? Which activities, projects, and stakeholders deserve the most attention if the firm is going to achieve its objectives? A big part of the prioritization task is determining *who* deserves attention and how much. This section focuses primarily on who deserves attention. Sections 5 and 6 will deal with the "how much" question.

A short answer to the "who" question is that all of a firm's stakeholders deserve attention. This does not mean that every manager is responsible for every stakeholder. It does mean that every stakeholder should be accounted for in the information gathering, planning, and decision processes of the firm (Freeman et al., 2007a). In Section 1 we defined stakeholders as groups and individuals who have a *valid* interest (a stake) in the activities and outcomes of a firm and whom the firm relies on in order to achieve its objectives. The word "valid" in this definition helps to eliminate many potential stakeholders, as does the qualification that the firm must rely on them to some extent.

The concept of stakeholders implies a two-way relationship, at a minimum. It is actually even more complex, because in reality stakeholders interact with each other, and the firm sits at the center of an interconnected value-creating network (Rowley, 1997). Nonetheless, in the interest of succinctness, given the brevity of this Element, we are going to focus primarily on bidirectional relationships between the firm and its stakeholders.

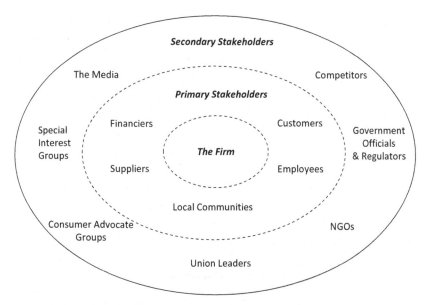

Figure 1 A basic stakeholder map.

3.1 Primary and Secondary Stakeholders

A basic stakeholder map is found in Figure 1. Note that the primary and secondary stakeholders do not have clear boundaries, and even the boundary between primary and secondary stakeholders is semipermeable (denoted by dotted lines).

3.1.1 Primary Stakeholders and Value Creation

Primary stakeholders are directly involved in the value-creating processes of the firm. This gives them an economic stake. For example, financiers such as banks require repayment of loans and shareholders expect price appreciation and dividends, employees expect competitive remuneration and job security, local communities demand taxes, customers expect a product or service with economic value at least equal to what they paid, and suppliers demand to be paid for what they provide to the firm. Of course, economic benefit is not the only value that is created for stakeholders. For example, a primary stakeholder may get emotional satisfaction through affiliating with a particular company, or the company could provide security, respect, political influence, knowledge, or network connections (Freeman, 1984; Harrison and Wicks, 2013). In turn, because they contribute to the creation of value, the firm depends on these stakeholders. They can also exhibit a very strong influence on firm decisions

(Frooman, 1999). Thus, there is a strong two-way relationship, and a concern for both fairness and managerial effectiveness suggests that these stakeholders should be given ample attention by management (Freeman et al., 2007a; Phillips, 2003; Mitchell et al., 1997). They are best treated as partners in value creation rather than adversaries or neutral parties with which the firm simply exchanges goods and services (Harrison and John, 1996; Jones et al., 2018).

3.1.2 What Is a Firm?

Perhaps a point of clarification would be helpful. In Figure 1 employees are not drawn inside the firm. If a business firm is not composed of its employees, than what is it? In this Element we use the word "firm" to describe a mechanism for organizing and directing stakeholder resources and actions so that value is created and then allocated fairly to stakeholders, which includes employees. The firm's managers have direct responsibility for these value-creating activities. And, as we said in Section 1, this Element is focused on business firms, although stakeholder theory can also be applied to other types of organizations.

3.1.3 The Importance of Secondary Stakeholders

Having defined the firm and its primary stakeholders, how do secondary stakeholders fit in and how do they qualify as stakeholders? Secondary stakeholders typically have what might be called an "influencer" stake in the firm (Freeman, 1984). This means they are not engaged directly in *value-creating* processes, but they do have a legitimate interest in what the firm does. They may well influence and affect the interests of primary stakeholders. For instance, consumer advocate groups have an interest in the quality and safety of the firm's products and services and how the firm treats its customers. That is their mission, which makes their interest legitimate even if it does not create value per se. The media serves as a "watch dog" reflecting societal interests and the need for transparency in the firm's operations. Government officials and regulators can be primary stakeholders to the extent that sometimes they partner with firms in creating value for stakeholders, but typically they simply collect tax revenues and set and enforce rules by which firms operate. Secondary stakeholders have an influencer stake because although they do not typically participate directly in the creation of value, their influence can help or hurt the ability of the firm in the achievement of its value-creating objectives (Eesley and Lenox, 2006; Freeman et al., 2007a; Su and Tsang, 2015). For instance, a special-interest group, especially if it is adept at working with the media, can hurt a firm's reputation, which can influence sales and the attractiveness of a firm to potential employees and other stakeholders with which the firm might want to engage.

As a result of their potential for influence, many firms are now partnering with secondary stakeholders; for instance, a well-organized NGO can influence government regulations. Union leaders can dramatically alter the competitiveness of a firm through their influence on wages, benefits, and other working conditions. Of course, the media, unions, special interests, and NGOs can also have a positive influence on a firm's reputation (Doh and Guay, 2006). For this reason, firms should pay attention to these stakeholders and should look for ways to cooperate with them whenever possible in the creation of value for stakeholders. For example, secondary stakeholders sometimes possess very useful information that can help a firm create more value.

Competitors are a special type of secondary stakeholder because their actions have so much influence on the outcomes of the firm and its ability to achieve its objectives. As we will discuss in Sections 5 and 6, this power sometimes makes it highly advantageous for firms to find ways to partner with them. For instance, a firm may engage in a joint research and development program with a competitor. Government officials and regulators also have a great deal of influence on a firm's activities and outcomes. Fostering good relationships with these stakeholders is therefore very important.

3.2 Identification of Specific Stakeholders

Grouping stakeholders into broad categories is a useful starting point in identifying stakeholders. It can be helpful to group stakeholders into categories such as "suppliers" or "customers" because they share common interests based on their functions in the value-creating process, and assigning them into groups can make decision making less complicated. For example, it may be helpful to consider customers as a whole when defining basic principles for how customers will be treated. However, the truth is that stakeholder interests are not completely homogeneous within these broad groups. Managing stakeholders is not that simple. To be more practical, the stakeholder framework must identify specific stakeholders and their needs and interests (McVea and Freeman, 2005). This allows the firm to adapt its plans and actions around particular stakeholders.

As an example of this finer level of identification, instead of using a broad grouping such as financiers, the firm might use categories such as bondholders, domestic banks, foreign banks, Class A stockholders, and Class B stockholders. Instead of customers, useful classifications could include families, singles, repeat customers, and business customers. As an alternative, customers could be segmented based on age groups, regions in which they live, or other demographic or sociocultural factors. Secondary stakeholders deserve this sort of segmentation also. Instead of competitors, a firm might find useful a classification such as price competitors, product competitors, quality competitors, or innovation competitors (Freeman et al., 2007a).

Moving to this more specific level of categorization, the firm is acknowledging that *all stakeholders* have customer-like power (mentioned in Section 1), in that they have a choice of whether and when to engage with the firm (Freeman, 1984; Harrison and Wicks, 2013). The firm is generalizing a very basic marketing approach of segmenting customers based on common needs, features, or interests. Of course, there might be different stakeholder maps for different businesses that are part of a multibusiness firm. The appropriate level for mapping stakeholders is the level at which strategies are established for managing those stakeholders in the value-creating process.

Beyond even these more specific classifications, stakeholders also have names and faces (McVea and Freeman, 2005). For example, a specific firm may sell its products to Walmart and Target, and through Amazon. The more traditional retailers are very different from the online giant Amazon in terms of their processes, needs, and interests. A supplier should account for these differences.

As another example, a manufacturer may receive its operating capital from SunTrust Bank, while more than half of its bonds are held by Chinese investors. With regard to shareholders, 10% of the company's stock is held by the retirement investment business of TIAA-CREF, 5% is held by a hedge fund, and the rest is widely distributed. These financiers are likely to have very different interests that are guiding their decisions with regard to the firm. These interests should be accounted for. The same logic applies to all of a firm's stakeholders.

The construction of stakeholder maps at the level of detail recommended in this section is not an easy task. The diagrams, tables, or other methods for listing all of the stakeholders within groups are going to be complicated. In addition, three other considerations make the task even more difficult. First, the stakeholders identified at a particular point in time are not a fixed set (Freeman et al., 2007a). They change regularly, with new stakeholders entering and existing stakeholders discontinuing their associations with the firm. Second, some stakeholders play more than one role (Freeman, 1984). A firm could have a customer that also supplies certain parts, or an employee could also be a shareholder. Third, some stakeholders are interconnected, as when a bank provides financing to two competing firms or to a firm and one of its suppliers. Another example would be a union that is closely tied to a special-interest group or NGO.

Given all of the complexities and challenges associated with identifying stakeholders, let alone trying to use this information to manage value-creating processes, is it possible to get anything valuable from doing so? In other words, do advantages outweigh the costs associated with this sort of activity? The reality is that value-creating systems are incredibly complex. We cannot escape this complexity, and oversimplifying the systems to facilitate decision-making processes means that many additional value-creating opportunities will be missed (best case scenario); the firm will more often make poor decisions that reduce stakeholder value (medium case scenario); and/or the firm may even go out of business, thus destroying much of the value for stakeholders (worst case scenario).

Think about the complexity of flying a jet between London and Tokyo. Would you get on that jet if there were not dozens or more systems in place, both in the jet and on the ground, to observe, collect, analyze, and transmit information to guide it safely through its journey? Would you get on that jet if you did not believe that the pilot would pay attention to that information? And does all that information collection, analysis, and transmission cost money? Of course it does, but it is worth the cost, right? Why, then, is it a good idea for investors to give their money to a firm that flies blind with regard to its customers, suppliers, communities, or to what an important special-interest group is doing?

Of course, no firm flies completely blind because it learns as it interacts with stakeholders. It is really a matter of the degree to which the firm deliberately and systematically identifies stakeholders, collects information from them, and uses that information in managing the value-creating processes of the firm. In our experience, firms that manage for stakeholders spend more time and other resources identifying stakeholders, assessing their interests, and using that information to provide strategic direction, determine firm attitudes and actions, and make both long- and shorter-term decisions, even regarding daily operations. Fortunately, large, complex businesses also have many resources and processes at their disposal for managing stakeholders and the value creation system to which they belong. Yes, it is possible to engage effectively in the processes associated with managing for stakeholders, and there is empirical evidence to suggest that doing so creates more value for stakeholders (i.e., Bettinazzi and Zollo, 2017; Choi and Wang, 2009; Henisz et al., 2014; Sisodia et al., 2007).

3.3 Stakeholders Are People

Stakeholders are people. They have emotions, biases, desires, needs, and interests. They also have varied experiences, cognitive capabilities, perspectives, skills, and backgrounds. In other words, people are complicated, although much of the popular thinking about business seems to assume the opposite. For example, many economics-based business models are founded on an assumption that humans are consistently rational, even though both research and anecdotal evidence suggests they are not. Closely associated with this notion is the assumption that people are completely self-interested (Bosse and Phillips, 2016). Following from this assumption, firms should feel compelled to use numerous safeguards when they interact with stakeholders in the form of long, detailed contracts and tight security on everything, including carefully guarded information and restricted access to other value-creating resources. These sorts of constraints, however, also reduce the ability of stakeholders to contribute to value-creating processes because they may not have access to the information and other resources needed to do so, or the freedom to do things that are not specified by a contract (Davis et al., 1997). They are limited. Also, the assumption of narrow self-interest can be self-reinforcing – when people are treated as though they are self-interested they begin to act that way.

We are not suggesting that people do not have any degree of self-interest, and that all information and resources should be shared with everyone, nor are we suggesting that contracts are never necessary. But what if we started with the assumption that people have an urge to create things of value for and with other people? Indeed, voluntary effort is the only reason that capitalism works as well as it does (Freeman et al., 2007b). This is not to deny the economic reality of an employee receiving a paycheck, or of a supplier getting paid. But how much money could be saved if a firm did not have to create and enforce such elaborate protection mechanisms (Jones, 1995; Jones et al., 2018)? Contracts, when really necessary, could be shorter and simpler. People would voluntarily work together to create more value. This assumption of voluntary cooperation in the creation of value is one of the essential assumptions of stakeholder management (Freeman et al., 2010). Section 4 explains why it works – that is, it provides the behavioral theory that explains why firms that manage for stakeholders create more value, even for shareholders!

4 How Stakeholder Management Works

In Section 1 we used an analogy of a pie to introduce the concept that increasing the value provided to one stakeholder does not necessarily mean that value to other stakeholders will be reduced. This is because the size of the pie is not fixed. The purpose of this section is to explain why managing for stakeholders increases the size of the pie. We will revisit and more carefully explain many of the core concepts introduced in Section 1, and how they are linked to value creation. We begin by explaining what we mean by managing for stakeholders. We will then define what we mean by total value creation. Finally, we will link managing for stakeholders to total value creation.

4.1 Managing for Stakeholders

This whole Element is about managing for stakeholders. What precisely does this involve? Here is a succinct set of descriptors for the behavior that these sorts of firms display.

1. They show integrity: they say what they mean and mean what they say. In other words, they are trustworthy.
2. They care about the welfare of their stakeholders. They are "other-regarding." They realize that everything they do should serve stakeholders in some way.
3. They understand that the purpose of a business is to create value for stakeholders, and their behavior is consistent with this purpose.
4. They engage in open, useful conversations with stakeholders (both primary and secondary stakeholders).
5. They are generous in rewarding stakeholders materially and in other ways, especially those who contribute the most to the value-creating processes of the firm.
6. They seek to align the interests of multiple stakeholders over time, as opposed to trading off the interests of one stakeholder against another. They find solutions to issues that satisfy these multiple stakeholders simultaneously.

Perhaps more should be said about attribute 6, because this is something that many managers have difficulty fully accepting. Seeing stakeholder interests as conjoint rather than in opposition to each other does not come naturally (Freeman et al., 2007b). However, we believe that a firm that constantly trades off the interests of one group against another is setting itself up for trouble and possibly even failure over the longer term. Often the wrong questions are being asked: "Why not cut employee benefits a little so we can invest in a new inventory system?" or "How can we reduce the costs of materials (which may reduce product quality) so that we can increase profits and dividends?" Instead of these sorts of questions, we suggest something like: "How can we restructure the way we manage the employee relationship so that employees are happier and more productive, thus resulting in higher profitability and the ability to pay more dividends?" Along these lines, Section 5 will provide some tools to help firms discover what is most important to stakeholders and Section 6 contains guidance for how to turn that stakeholder intelligence into strategies that create more value for stakeholders.

Publix Supermarkets, Inc. is an excellent example of a company that manages for stakeholders (Harrison et al., 2018). George Jenkins started Publix in Winter Haven, Florida in 1930, after having had a bad experience as a manager at a different grocery chain. He resolved to create a different kind of grocer – a company that provides superior customer service and takes excellent care of its employees. He did it, and Publix is now the largest employee-owned company in America. Being employee-owned immediately aligns employee and shareholder interests. Employees are surveyed annually for feedback on policies, leadership, business practices, and compensation packages. The company recruits managers from within, and its employee turnover is a small fraction of the turnover rates of competitors. It has been listed on Fortune's 100 Best Companies to Work for in America for more than a decade. With regard to customers, the company's motto is, "Where Shopping Is a Pleasure," and it has ranked first among supermarkets on the American Customer Satisfaction Index for many years. In addition, Publix has been identified as one of the most socially responsible companies in America. The additional costs associated with the company's stakeholder-oriented policies and practices are more than offset by the additional value the firm co-creates with them. In fact, Publix now has revenues of more than $34 billion and more than 1,000 stores in multiple states, with substantially more growth expected.

4.2 Total Stakeholder Value

Historically, business executives, investors, and even business scholars have been obsessed with economic measures of the value a firm creates (Stout, 2012). This is natural because it is relatively easy to measure economic outcomes when compared to the other types of value a firm creates (Harrison and Wicks, 2013). However, an entrepreneur seldom sets out to make money by making money. A product or service is the vehicle for making money, and it is the value that a customer gets from the product or service that makes positive economic outcomes possible. In this sense, financial figures such as sales or profits serve as proxies for how much value a firm is creating, but these proxies may be far removed from the actual utility the customer receives. For example, a customer may pay $10 for a product, but after using it a while, may feel as though it would have been worth $100 or perhaps $5. The difference typically comes only in part from the perceived economic benefits of the product. Often other noneconomic factors are just as important.

The truth is that is it hard to measure actual utility received by stakeholders through their interactions and transactions with the firm, but that does not mean firms should simply abandon the concept and rely exclusively on economic measures of value. Of course, firms should not completely abandon economic measures either because businesses require financial capital to survive. In Section 4.2.1 we will explore noneconomic types of value that are commonly created (or destroyed) by the operations of business firms, and in Section 7 we will provide some ideas for how to measure these types of stakeholder value.

4.2.1 Noneconomic Sources of Value for Stakeholders

As just explained, the actual amount of value customers receive from the products and services of a firm is not perfectly correlated with what they pay for them. The fact that all stakeholders have customer-like power means that they decide whether to engage with a firm based on their own perceptions of the value they provide to the firm versus the value they receive from the firm, all in the context of their opportunity cost, or what they could get from engaging with a competing firm. Their own perceptions of the value they receive include noneconomic sources of value. For example, an employee may get an annual salary of $40,000 per year and what she perceives as excellent benefits in exchange for working 40 hours per week at Instinct Inc. Furthermore, she believes that she would make about the same at a competing firm in the industry but her benefits would not be as good. So she stays. Just like a customer, she is trading something of value (40 hours of effort per week) for something of value.

But it isn't really as simple as this example suggests. Consider a situation in which the employee is given an offer of $50,000 per year and the same level of benefits by a competing firm in the same town (which means there will not be any moving costs), and, in fact, the firm is closer to her home so her commute would be reduced. Will she go? We don't know. The answer may depend on factors that have not yet been mentioned in this example. These are other types of value she receives from working with Instinct Inc. One of these factors may be value through affiliation. She may feel really good about working for Instinct Inc. because they are good corporate citizens – they have a strong sustainability program and allow employees to work at local homeless shelters once a month while continuing to receive their regular salaries. She may enjoy working with others at the company who share her values and who help her grow and develop. She may also believe in the growth potential of the company, and trust that as it grows her salary will grow too. Or she may just really like working there because of the respect with which she is treated, the opportunities she has to participate in important decisions, and the challenge of her job that makes her feel as though she is developing as a human being.

Many of us work for firms that pay us a salary that is substantially below what we believe we could receive elsewhere because of value we receive from affiliation, trust, respect, personal development, or security. In fact, when we receive this sort of value from a firm, we are also more prone to exhibit behaviors such as loyalty and higher levels of motivation and performance (Bosse and Coughlan, 2016; Bosse et al., 2009; Hosmer, 1994; Jones, 1995).

The same sort of logic applies to other stakeholders. Customers may buy a product because they believe in the company. They feel great about displaying the company logo on the product they have bought. A customer may wear a shirt that proudly displays "Harley-Davidson" on the front or a carry a laptop computer that says "Intel inside" on the cover. In an episode of *The Simpsons* television program, School Superintendent Chalmers bought a Honda Accord, and the "H" was stolen off the front. He lamented, "That's how people know it's a Honda. What's the point of having a Honda if you can't show it off?" Suppliers also can experience feelings of affiliation or happiness as a result of the respect and integrity with which they are treated. Communities can feel proud to have a particular company in their neighborhood. A firm that manages for stakeholders knows what its stakeholders most value, and it diligently tries to satisfy those interests.

4.2.2 Organizational Justice and Total Value for Stakeholders

Organizational justice (e.g., fairness) explains much of the value a stakeholder receives from the firm (Bosse et al., 2009; Harrison et al., 2010). Procedural justice comes from a firm's behaviors that make a stakeholder feel as though his opinion counts and his interests are considered when managers make decisions and formulate strategies (Colquitt et al., 2001; Kim and Mauborgne, 1998). In many cases, firms deliberately collect information directly from stakeholders and engage them in conversation about a topic before making a decision, or even include them in decision processes when it is practical to do so. For example, a firm may ask community leaders to sit on a planning panel or suppliers to be involved with the design of a new product. This kind of inclusion can bring a great deal of satisfaction to stakeholders and thus increase the value they get from affiliating with the firm. Firms that exhibit a large degree of procedural justice have what might be called "close" relationships with their stakeholders, as opposed to arms-length relationships in which they merely exchange goods or services in an open market with very little information exchange or sharing of resources (Jones et al., 2018).

Interactional justice pertains to the way a firm treats its stakeholders on a day-to-day basis (Cropanzana et al., 2007). Firms that manage for stakeholders treat their stakeholders with respect and honesty. They have a mutually engaged relationship. If a misunderstanding occurs, it is resolved through open communication. In situations in which bad news has to be delivered, it is delivered directly to the stakeholder with a complete explanation. This sort of justice fosters open communication, which can motivate stakeholders to share valuable information and other resources with the firm.

Distributional justice occurs as stakeholders believe they are receiving a fair allocation of value from the firm for what they contribute to value-creating processes (Nelson, 2001; Rabin, 1993). As explained previously, this value can be economic, tangible (as in the utility received from a product or service), or intangible. Often stakeholders of firms that manage for stakeholders actually feel as though they are receiving more value than what they would really need to motivate them to do business with the firm, as demonstrated by a customer who believes she got a "great deal" on a product she bought. Combining these three forms of justice, we get a fairly complete picture of the total value a firm creates for its stakeholders.

It is also possible for a firm to destroy stakeholder value through disrespecting or otherwise mistreating stakeholders, ignoring their interests during decision-making processes, or allocating value to them that they perceive as unfair compared to what they contribute to the value-creating processes of the firm. Companies that exhibit behaviors that elicit these sorts of feelings among many of their primary stakeholders typically will not succeed for long. We also recognize that sometimes a company will deliberately underallocate value to a particular stakeholder (e.g., underpay employees, create poor quality products, or intentionally delay payments to suppliers) in order to enhance profitability, and they may even enjoy higher levels of profitability for a period of time.

We have two things to say about a strategy that deliberately mistreats stakeholders in the pursuit of increased profitability. First, those firms are not creating as much *total* value for stakeholders as they could, as the value received by employees or other stakeholders is relatively low, especially if you include intangible factors in addition to economic factors (Harrison and Wicks, 2013). Second, from a stakeholder perspective, the primary purpose of a firm is to create value for stakeholders (Freeman, 1984). Consequently, we consider those sorts of firms a failure. We also believe that, at least in industrialized countries, eventually these situations will be at least partially corrected through market or political forces (Stout, 2012). In this sense, firms that mistreat stakeholders to enhance short-term profits are pursuing high-risk strategies.

4.3 Managing for Stakeholders to Increase Total Value

In this section we will combine concepts from the previous two sections. How is it, specifically, that managing for stakeholders increases the total value a firm creates for its stakeholders?

We begin with a simple scenario and a question. Consider two competing firms, Firm A and Firm B, both with sales of $100 billion. Firm A has profits of $10 billion. Its customers love its products. Its employees feel very happy because they get to work with the firm. Its suppliers are frequently consulted about new product designs, something that makes them feel like part of the team. Communities feel pride at having one of Firm A's plants in their neighborhood. Firm B also has profits of $10 billion. Its customers find its products acceptable to meet their purposes, but they don't feel any special bond with the company. Its employees put in their hours of work, but they really look forward to going home each day. Employee turnover is higher than industry norms. Its suppliers have arms-length business transactions with the firm and are not consulted on new product designs. Communities tolerate the presence of their plants. One community leader said, "Well, at least they provide some tax revenue, which is nice." Which firm is creating more value?

Obviously, Firm A is creating more value, as long as we do not rely exclusively on profits to measure value. The numbers are not measuring total value accurately. Continuing with this example, the next question is how Firm A can do extra things that make its stakeholders so happy and still have a profit of $10 billion. Much of the additional value that is created to make up for the additional costs can be explained in terms of reciprocity (Bosse et al., 2009). As we mentioned previously, humans respond positively when they are treated well and negatively when they are treated poorly.

Reciprocity allows firms to gain net economic benefits from treating stakeholders well in spite of the additional outflows of time, money, and other resources (Harrison et al., 2010; Sisodia et al., 2007). Employees are likely to work harder and share valuable information that can enhance efficiency or innovation because they trust that the firm will listen to them, and any new value created as a result of their additional efforts or ideas will ultimately be allocated back to them in some form or other. Customers tend to exhibit loyalty, financiers may offer better terms, and communities can offer tax breaks or provide additional or improved infrastructure that enhances firm efficiency. These are just a few of an almost limitless list of possibilities.

Some of the benefits from fostering trusting, respectful, and mutually beneficial relationships with stakeholders include an excellent reputation and the ability to draw a larger number of value-creating stakeholders to the firm because it is so attractive to work with, and thus the ability to obtain better resources, especially valuable information (Barringer and Harrison, 2000; Freeman et al., 2010; Harrison et al., 2010). These benefits result in an enhanced ability to plan and a higher level of strategic flexibility because the firm can more easily obtain what it needs from a wider range of potential stakeholders (Freeman and Evan, 1990). In terms of value created, in addition to all the noneconomic value described in this section, the firm is likely to be more *efficient* because of the additional efforts of its stakeholders and more *innovative* because of the valuable information it receives from them. It should have higher sales growth because its customers are so happy with innovative products and the value proposition they receive (value/price). Such a firm tends to have an outstanding reputation and experience fewer negative stakeholder actions such as bad, press, lawsuits, or boycotts, which means less risk (Cornell and Shapiro, 1987; Graves and Waddock, 1994; Shane and Spicer, 1983).

Trust is essential to unlocking these value-creating benefits (Bridoux and Stoelhorst, 2016; Harrison et al., 2010; Jones et al., 2018). Stakeholders must trust that the information they give to the firm will be recognized and used appropriately, and that they will share in any new value created as a result of the information. They must feel as though their loyalty and additional efforts for the firm will be rewarded, and the firm will not intentionally take advantage of them. Because trust is so important, firms that manage for stakeholders must take quick action to resolve any actual or perceived breaches of trust and repair their relationships with the stakeholders affected. Also, one of the best ways to build trust with a stakeholder is to have a power differential or an information advantage or some other advantage over a stakeholder, and not use it. This is not uncommon for larger firms. They frequently have a great deal of power relative to that of many of their stakeholders. If they abstain from using it to the disadvantage of their stakeholders, they can engender a great deal of trust.

Returning to our pie example, a firm that manages for stakeholders is in a much better position to create more total value for stakeholders so that additional investments in stakeholders *now* are made possible because of stakeholder investments in the past. In other words, the stakeholder-oriented firm is constantly creating additional value and this value is then available to invest in stakeholders so that they will create even more additional value in the next business cycle. Managing for stakeholders works because the benefit/cost ratio tends to be positive, or, more accurately, the incremental benefits in time +1 exceed the incremental costs in time 0. Returning to our previous example, Publix allocates more resources to customer service, employee involvement and rewards, and community responsibility than its competitors do, but the benefits outweigh the additional costs. This does not mean there should not be any limits to the amount of value allocated to stakeholders. Rational limits to value allocations will be discussed in Section 7. It does mean that firms that manage for stakeholders create more value for stakeholders. In addition to substantial anecdotal evidence, there is a growing body of empirical evidence that shareholders are among the beneficiaries of this sort of management (i.e., Bettinazzi and Zollo, 2017; Choi and Wang, 2009; Henisz et al., 2014; Sisodia et al., 2007).

5 Tools for Understanding Stakeholders

One of the primary benefits of managing for stakeholders is obtaining superior information on which to make management decisions and develop strategies that unlock new sources of value creation. As described in Section 4, when stakeholders feel as though they are being treated well they are much more willing to share important information with the firm. This information can then be used to help the firm develop a strong mission, enterprise strategy, and values, as well as specific strategies that provide more value to stakeholders and give the firm a competitive edge. For the next few sections we will refer to this sort of information as stakeholder intelligence.

Luck Companies, a stakeholder-oriented firm and one of the largest aggregate manufacturers in the eastern United States, is a model for collecting this sort of intelligence. The company's deliberate purpose is to ensure the success of others, whether it is customers, each other (its own associates), other companies, or the community. Luck's representatives travel the world, literally, speaking about values-based leadership. Their entire management model is focused on values, and ensuring they are an integral part of everything they do. For example, they conduct what they call a 360 assessment in which leaders at all levels of the firm ask about a dozen or so people (from inside and outside the firm) to evaluate them based on the values of the firm. They listen, and they act on what they hear. This sort of management approach inspires stakeholders to provide valuable intelligence. For example, Luck has a program they call 9-Box, an ongoing anonymous process facilitated by an external consulting company that allows all associates to provide input about the company and their bosses. Almost all associates participate even though it is not required of them (Wicks and Harrison, 2015).

This section provides practical tools for gathering stakeholder intelligence, Section 6 adds methods for using stakeholder intelligence to create value, and Section 7 ties all the tools together by providing guidelines for developing stakeholder-based performance measures and a control system that helps ensure that objectives are met. Figure 2 lays out the section topics, with Section 5 topics in the top half of the figure and Section 6 topics in the bottom half. Remember that guidelines for identifying stakeholders (very top of figure) were provided in Section 3.

It is not necessary for a firm to use all of these stakeholder tools. In fact, in some cases a firm may already be very aware of the power of its various stakeholders, why they believe and act the way they do, what their interests are, what their current and potential contributions are, or the strategies the firm is currently using to manage them. On the other hand, it may be that there are some important blind spots. Our recommendation is that managers choose the tools that are most important to their own unique situations. All of these tools have the potential to uncover important information and unlock new sources of value creation.

5.1 Assessment of Stakeholder Power

It is not uncommon for a firm to possess more power than one of its stakeholders because of its size, political connections, or the asymmetric information it may possess and, as mentioned in other sections, one of the ways a firm can build trust and loyalty is by not using this information to the disadvantage of that stakeholder. However, it is also common for a stakeholder to possess power, even great power, owing to a number of situational factors (Porter, 1980, 1985). We are using the word power to mean a stakeholder's capacity to influence the outcomes of a firm's decisions and strategies (Harrison and John, 1996). Awareness of the power of stakeholders helps a firm determine the nature of the strategies it should pursue with each of them. In general, the more

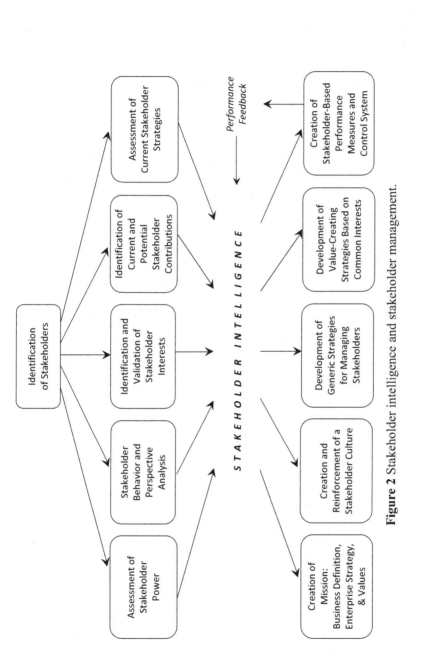

Figure 2 Stakeholder intelligence and stakeholder management.

power a stakeholder possesses, the more a firm should take actions to ensure that the stakeholder feels like a partner in value creation rather than a foe. This theme will be further developed, along with specific strategies for doing so, in Section 5.1.1.

Power can be assessed in general terms by looking at stakeholders in broader groups such as suppliers or customers, but it is frequently more useful to assess power at the individual "names-and-faces" level. This section will discuss how to assess the power of the most important stakeholders for most firms – customers, suppliers, employees, financiers, local communities, and competitors. The same criteria can be used whether a firm is assessing the power of an individual stakeholder or of a broader group of stakeholders. We begin by providing criteria to help a firm understand the economic power of its stakeholders.

5.1.1 Economic Power of Stakeholders

The economic power of stakeholders is influenced by a firm's dependence on the resources they provide to value creating processes. That is, resource dependence is foundational to many of the specific factors that give stakeholders economic power (Pfeffer and Salancik, 1978).

Economic Power of Customers. Although all customers are important, some have more economic power than others. Economic power can give stakeholders a great deal of influence over the decisions a firm makes and outcomes from those decisions (Frooman, 1999; Harrison and John, 1996). For instance, they can use economic power to dictate terms and conditions associated with the products and services they are buying, as well as their prices. However, they can also wield economic power to influence firms in areas such as governance, corporate responsibility, information disclosure, employee treatment, and choice of suppliers. Typically customers have more economic power if any or all of several conditions are present:

1. They are few in number, which means the firm cannot afford to lose one.
2. They make high-volume purchases, which produces an economic dependence.
3. The products they are buying from the firm are widely available from other firms.
4. They have better information about the firm they are buying from than the firm has about them. For example, the customer may know precisely the raw materials and production costs that go into a product, whereas the firm does

not have reliable information about the real value of the product to the customer.

5. It is easy for a customer to switch to another supplier of the product or service. There are low switching costs. Some companies, such as IBM, built their business on the notion of making their products unique so it is hard for a customer to switch to a different vendor (Porter, 1980, 1985).

Economic Power of Suppliers. Suppliers with a high level of economic power can influence uncertainty through the prices they charge; the terms they require; the level of service they offer; and the nature, quality, and availability of the products and services they provide. The following factors, many of which mirror the customer factors, give suppliers economic power:

1. Only one or a few suppliers provide what the firm needs.
2. They do not depend much on the firm for a large portion of their sales. They are not economically dependent.
3. The characteristics of the product or service the supplier provides are essential to the value the firm creates. This is especially true if a supplier provides products and services that are highly differentiated.
4. They have better information about the firm they are selling to than the firm has about them.
5. They have made it costly to switch to other sources of supply (Porter, 1980, 1985).

Economic Power of Employees. Great employees are critical to the ability of the firm to create value, and they can also possess a high level of economic power under certain conditions. Factors that tend to give an employee economic power include the following:

1. There is a shortage of workers in the area in which the firm needs them.
2. Worker skills and experience are highly differentiated, and the firm needs a particular skill set that an employee possesses to create value through its activities.
3. Competitors are aggressively pursuing the most valuable employees with attractive employment offers.
4. Employees have abundant information about the firm's operations, information systems, proprietary information, and profitability.
5. It is difficult or expensive to provide the additional training needed to produce in-house employees that possess the requisite skills.

There is frequently a great deal of power variance across particular employees, even within the same company location. For example, Disney hires a large number of low-skilled employees for its theme parks. It pays them very low wages and frequently gives them unattractive work schedules and difficult or tedious work assignments, yet it has no trouble recruiting new employees because so many people want to work at a fun place like Disney World. On the other hand, Disney theme parks also employ a group of highly skilled, talented performing artists. These people have more economic power because their skills and experience are highly differentiated, and it would be difficult for Disney to give them the training in-house that they would need to perform certain tasks. Consequently, Disney considers and treats these people differently, including their compensation.

Economic Power of Financiers. With regard to value creation, financiers include primarily banks and other financial institutions that provide a great deal of the operating capital for firms. These financiers can also include firms that facilitate the sale of bonds or the bondholders themselves. These types of stakeholders are a central part of the value-creating process precisely because they provide needed operating capital, and especially if the firm intends to grow, which is part of creating new value for stakeholders. Financiers have more economic power under the following conditions:

1. The firm is young and does not have a strong financial track record yet.
2. The industry in which the firm is competing is considered unstable, new, or otherwise unattractive.
3. There are not many financiers interested in making loans or investments in the particular industry segment or to the firm.
4. The firm has had some financial difficulties in the past.
5. The firm is already highly leveraged, which makes it a riskier investment.

Shareholders are different from other types of financiers (Stout, 2012). After a shareholder buys a share of stock, thus providing needed capital, he or she is pretty much out of the picture with regard to the value-creating activities of the firm. That is, he or she does not participate in these processes on an ongoing and regular basis. If the firm works with its other stakeholders to create more value, the shareholders should be happy because the stock should perform well. This means also that the share price should be relatively high, which makes the company an attractive investment if it decides to issue more shares of stock.

After the shares are bought, most shareholders have very little economic power because shares of stock tend to be widely distributed. The exception to this rule occurs when an individual shareholder or investing institution purchases a large block of stock. Large-block shareholders have more power than individual shareholders because they can influence stock prices by selling off their shares of stock. In some cases, they may even threaten to buy out the rest of the corporation through a tender offer. These factors give large-block shareholders power, which is sometimes manifest in strategic planning processes, board meetings, and through direct communications with managers; however, in our experience managers often give too much credence to this power, and it causes them to take a short-term profit maximizing perspective that destroys value. Our recommendation is not to ignore shareholder interests, but to not let them dictate decisions that destroy value or prevent decisions that can create more value for stakeholders. Again, shareholders do very little to *participate* in ongoing value-creating processes. In many ways, they become more like a secondary "influencer" stakeholder after their shares are purchased.

Economic Power of Local Communities. When we consider the community stakeholder as a group, we are talking primarily about the leaders of local government, political, and social organizations that most influence the local operating environment for the firm. Communities can be central to creating value because they provide much of the infrastructure a firm needs to operate (Freeman et al., 2007a). In addition, the attractiveness of a community can attract or deter potential employees. Perhaps even more important, local communities can influence the "rules of the game" through regulation and taxation. In general, communities have a great deal of economic power under the following conditions:

1. They are in a prime, unique location for the business activities of the firm because of proximity to suppliers, customers, distribution channels, employees with special skills, educational institutions, or for some other firm-specific reason.
2. Other firms, which may include competitors, are highly interested in locating within that particular community.
3. Community leaders have accurate and abundant information about the firm's operations, policies, employment, and profitability.
4. The firm is experiencing significant growth and must therefore expand its operations.
5. The structure of local taxation is easily changed. This can happen, for instance, if the voters in the community have a record of regularly supporting new tax initiatives.
6. A firm's leases or other location-specific contracts are about to expire.

Economic Power of Competitors. Although we tend to look at competitors as secondary stakeholders, they can also have a great deal of economic power

(Porter, 1980, 1985). Economically powerful competitors can wield their power through strategies such as aggressive innovation or marketing programs, poaching valuable employees from other firms, or price cutting. Competition is a more powerful force in industries that are growing slowly and in those that have high fixed costs, very little product differentiation, or high exit barriers (what you lose if you leave the industry). Oligopolies, in which only a few firms control most of the sales, contain large firms with a great deal of economic power. There are many factors that can give a competitor economic power (Freeman et al., 2007a; Porter, 1980, 1985; Wasserman and Faust, 1994). We list here only a few of the most common.

1. They are large and therefore possess numerous resources with which they can overwhelm their competitors.
2. The resources they possess are rare, such as unusually good locations or superior technology that is hard to imitate and/or legally protected through patents.
3. They have a strong reputation established over a long time period. The reputation is frequently associated with an especially strong brand image combined with a logo or trademark (e.g., Coke, Nike, Disney).
4. They have unusually strong and beneficial relationships, particularly with stakeholders who possess knowledge or other resource of great value. They may also have long-term contracts with these stakeholders, providing exclusive rights over an extended period of time.
5. They possess *network centrality*, in that they are leaders at the center of an interdependent network of companies that work together to create value.
6. They are aggressive in their strategies and willing to take risks.
7. They are extremely well connected politically (which leads us to our next source of power).

5.1.2 Political Power of Stakeholders

Although economic power is important, it is not the only kind of power a stakeholder may possess. Political power comes from the ability of a stakeholder to influence the political process in its favor and/or against the firm (Cummings and Doh, 2000; Freeman, 1984). Lobbying, political contributions, family relationships, or long-time friendships with politicians; alliances with political parties, public relations and advertising, or membership in industry associations; and support from interest groups, activists, or NGOs can enhance a stakeholder's political power. This sort of power is available to any of a firm's stakeholders, and firms are wise to acknowledge it in their planning and decision-making processes.

An illustration of the influence of political power, at a group level, exists in the automobile industry in the United States. One might think that the large manufacturers possess a great ability to influence regulation in the industry. Because of their size, lobbying, and political contributions they are not powerless; however, when issues put the big manufacturers in conflict with automobile dealers, it is a different matter. This is because the big manufacturers are concentrated in particular parts of the nation, and those areas are represented by few legislators in Congress compared with the dealers, who are totally spread out across the nation and have representatives in each of their areas. Furthermore, the National Automobile Dealers Association is large, well organized, and powerful in its own right. So for issues in which the interests of dealers conflict with those of the automobile manufacturers, the dealers may actually have the most political power in some cases, and thus the greater ability to influence the rules of the game.

5.1.3 Social Influence of Stakeholders

Some stakeholders are very adept at influencing public opinion, whether or not they have other types of political power (Cummings and Doh, 2000; Friedman, 1999; Frooman, 1999; Schrempf, 2012; Schrempf-Stirling et al., 2013). Social influence is sometimes considered a part of the general category of political power, but in some ways it is actually more pervasive in terms of its ability to affect a broader group of stakeholders. Regardless, it has become so influential that it deserves its own category.

Stakeholders may have power to influence public opinion owing to their expertise with the press or social media, their alliances with other stakeholders, the strength of their cause in the eyes of society, or the support of an interest group, activist, or NGO. Some of the common manifestations of an unhappy stakeholder with a great deal of social influence include boycotts, walkouts and strikes, damaged reputations, lost sales, community resistance to plant expansions, reduced share prices, or lost contracts with other stakeholders. Of course, a stakeholder with much social influence might also use this influence in the form of political power in an effort to change the rules through new regulations or through government sanctions or lawsuits. Ignoring stakeholders with a great deal of social influence can be hazardous. To the extent possible, a firm that manages for stakeholders will attempt to make such a stakeholder an ally rather than an adversary. Then its skill in swaying public opinion can be value producing instead of value destroying.

5.1.4 Legitimate, Contractual, or Institutionally Based
Sources of Power

In addition to economic, political, and social influence based power, stakeholders can possess power based on a variety of other factors that are specific to their own unique contexts. One of these sources is often called legitimate power, which comes from a formal position or office held within or without the firm, the possession of which gives the stakeholder certain rights (Freeman, 1984). For instance, a CEO has certain powers because of her or his position, and these powers will vary depending on the firm. The mayor of a local community will also possess powers that could influence firm outcomes.

Similar to legitimate power, stakeholders may also have certain rights granted to them through existing contracts with the firm. The legal system provides an opportunity for remedies if contracts are not fulfilled, which gives stakeholders contractual power.

Another form of power comes from the institutions to which firms belong. An institution, in this sense, is a group of firms that are engaged in the same line of business and pursue many of the same customers. For example, accounting firms form an institution. Firms that belong to an institution experience pressures to conform to particular norms and practices, some of them a result of tradition as the institution developed and some of them a result of societal expectations (DiMaggio and Powell, 1983). These norms can give stakeholders power. For example, in higher education it is expected that if a professor is going to be terminated, she or he will be given an entire year to find another job unless there are extreme situations such as commission of a crime. Often this is not a contractual obligation, but rather a norm that is adhered to by members of the institution of higher education.

The kind of power shareholders possess can best be described as legitimate power combined with a broad form of institutional power, where the institution is the group of corporations that have widely distributed shares of stock (e.g., not family owned). Their legitimate power comes from their voting rights and their ability to attend board meetings and place shareholder proposals before the board in those meetings. Shareholder activists have taken advantage of these rights, with some success, especially if they can draw the attention of the business press. However, much of shareholder power is institutional (Heminway, 2017). Society believes shareholders have power. Business people believe they have power. Many lawyers and judges believe they have power. So they have power. It is an institutional norm. Nonetheless, as we suggested previously, we believe that managers should minimize the influence of short-termism on their decisions, which is often associated with a focus on shareholder wealth maximization, and instead focus on how to create more value for stakeholders over the long *and* shorter terms.

To summarize, stakeholders with a great deal of social influence or economic, political, legitimate, contractual, and/or institutionally based power can have a large impact on the value-creating activities of the firm. They produce much uncertainty for the firm's managers and, as Section 5.2 will explain, should be given special attention during the development of mission, culture, and value-creating strategies. The basic idea is that rather than looking at a powerful stakeholder as an enemy that needs to be guarded against, that stakeholder should be seen as a partner in value creation. We will develop this idea further in Section 6.

5.2 Stakeholder Behavior and Perspective Analysis

An understanding of stakeholder power can help a firm anticipate stakeholder behavior to some degree; that is, a stakeholder with a great deal of power is likely to behave differently in its interactions with the firm than one with little power. However, it may be helpful also to identify specific stakeholder behaviors, or possible future behaviors, in terms of their value creating or harmful potential. In addition, while most managers believe they understand why stakeholders are behaving in a particular way, firms should dig deeper to understand their perspectives in more depth. Both of these analysis techniques can help a firm engage with stakeholders in a more productive and value-creating way.

5.2.1 Segmenting Stakeholder Behavior

Managers who interact directly with stakeholders need to think through the range of stakeholder reactions and behaviors. Many have found it useful to identify a stakeholder's current behaviors and then to think through how changes in those behaviors can help the firm or, alternatively, how changes could hurt the firm (Freeman et al., 2007a). Segmenting stakeholder behavior into these categories can lead to a more in-depth understanding of the value creation process.

The first category, current behavior, asks the manager to set forth those behaviors that describe the current state of the relationship between the firm and the stakeholder on the issue in question. For example, an important employee issue may be productivity or a supplier issue could be quality of parts provided. Current behavior may even describe responses to existing strategies for dealing with these issues, where such programs are underway.

The second category of behavior, cooperative potential, asks the manager to list concrete behaviors that could be observed in the future that would help the firm achieve a higher objective on the issue in question. Or, what could a stakeholder group do to assist the firm to create more value? Cooperative potential sets forth the best of all possible worlds in terms of what a stakeholder could do to help. It represents the changes in actual behavior that would be more helpful in the business in which the firm competes.

The third and final category of behavior, potentially harmful or threatening behavior, asks the manager to list those actions a stakeholder could take that would reduce the amount of value a firm creates or in other ways prevent it from achieving one or more of its goals. By thinking through what a stakeholder could do to hurt a firm, a manager can understand the downside risks associated with managing that stakeholder. By examining cooperative potential and potentially harmful behavior, the firm can take specific actions that seek to maximize the former and prevent the latter.

For managers who deal with stakeholders every day and who have an intuitive sense of how a stakeholder can help or hurt the business, this tool adds nothing new. By focusing on behavior, it asks executives not to immediately jump to wondering if a stakeholder is for or against them, but to focus on the value creation process and ask what behavior must occur for value creation to take place. For many firms that define their stakeholders to include groups outside the day-to-day operations of the business, thinking through concrete behaviors can be a useful prelude to dialogue and engagement.

5.2.2 Understanding Stakeholder Perspectives

Each of us sees the world from our own point of view—from a mindset that we have developed consciously and unconsciously over our entire lives. We make assumptions about the way the world works, about what makes a business successful, and about what makes other people tick. Often we aren't even aware of these assumptions. Communicating with others who have different perspectives on the world is a difficult, yet crucial stakeholder management task. It is easy to claim that a stakeholder we find difficult to work with is being irrational or acting on emotion, especially when there is much at stake.

Whenever we are tempted to declare that a stakeholder is acting irrationally or "wrong," we should try substituting the phrase, "I just don't understand that stakeholder's point of view." It may be that a stakeholder's interests are different from those of the firm, or there may be external forces influencing the stakeholder, or the stakeholder may be motivated by a different set of values. Wouldn't it be nice to understand these things? We believe that there is no conflict that cannot be resolved if both parties to the conflict are willing to assume the other's perspective. Understanding a stakeholder's perspective makes a firm much more effective at understanding the behavior of, communicating with, and working with that stakeholder, and potentially addressing that stakeholder's interests.

In our experience, asking a simple set of questions can help a firm understand a stakeholder's perspective, thus resulting in more effective strategies (Freeman et al., 2007a):

1. What are this stakeholder's main interests? How do we affect these interests? How are we affected by these interests?
2. Who are the groups and individuals who can affect this stakeholder? Who are the stakeholder's stakeholders? And what is the stake (interest) of each?
3. What do the members of this group probably believe about us? What assumptions are they making? What assumptions do we make about them?
4. What are the natural coalitions that could occur? Where are the joint interests? What do we and the stakeholder have in common? What are the major points of conflict?
5. What might cause a stakeholder to engage in behavior that is more cooperative? More harmful?

There is no "right" set of questions that works for all stakeholders under all circumstances, but these questions are a good start. Answering these questions is the same as constructing a theory about why stakeholders act the way they do and how their behavior might be expected to change. Managers have to put themselves in the stakeholder's place and try to empathize with that stakeholder's position. They must try to feel what the stakeholder feels and see the world from the stakeholder's perspective. It is not necessary to agree with the stakeholder's point of view; however, assuming the position of a stakeholder allows the manager to more fully understand that stakeholder's behavior, and how to respond to it in a way that minimizes potential harm to the firm and works toward a cooperative relationship with the stakeholder that allows more value to be created.

5.2.3 Identification and Validation of Stakeholder Interests

A recent research study was both fascinating and validating (Retolaza et al., 2015). The researchers conducted field research on stakeholder interests over a two-year period in two stages. In the first stage, they collected data from 304 agents associated with Euskalit, a foundation grouping more than 700 companies in the Basque Country of Spain. They asked these agents to identify the interests of all of the relevant stakeholders of the companies with which they were affiliated. Surprisingly, only twenty-three interests were identified. They included things like product and service improvements, long-term survival, improved working conditions, cash flow, and generation of social value outside the normal business activities of the firm. They then took these interests back to the original agents, and 96.8% of them agreed with the list, while the other 3.2% disagreed on only one item. To validate this list further, in the second stage the researchers sent it to the top executive responsible for the company's social responsibility area in each of the Spanish IBEX-35 firms. Of the thirty-two executives who responded, all agreed that twenty-two of the twenty-three interests were pertinent. Furthermore, when they were asked what was missing, they identified at most three interests not reflected in the table, all of which were specific to just one of the firms. We have since seen a presentation of another research project in which a large, but manageable set of stakeholder interests was identified.

We are sharing this research with you at the beginning of this section so that you can believe that what we are about to share with you is actually possible – it is not so complicated that it cannot be effectively implemented within a firm. In Section 3 we provided some guidance with regard to identifying stakeholders. As we suggested, analyzing the characteristics (i.e., power) of groups of stakeholders such as "customers" or "financiers" is useful for some strategic purposes, but it is better to work at the "names-and-faces" level when identifying interests. This is because the interests of stakeholders are likely to be different even within these broad categories. It may be that a corporate-level assessment of interests is relevant and useful, but any manager at any level in the firm can conduct an interests assessment that is relevant to her or his job.

Once key stakeholders have been determined (see Section 3), their primary interests should be identified. As in the case of Luck Companies, much of this information can come from managers and employees based on their interactions with stakeholders. Other valuable intelligence can come from historical records, from news stories featuring stakeholders, and from a myriad of stakeholder documents such as their annual reports, press releases, missions and values statements, and so forth. The Internet has made finding much of this type of information easier. However, managers may also need to communicate directly with stakeholders to determine what issues are most important to them.

		Stakeholders			
	Employees	Customers	Financiers	Suppliers	Community
Improved Products	3	1	2	2	4
Improved Working Conditions	1	5	5	4	2
Cash Flow	3	4	1	1	4
Social Value Added	3	3	5	4	1

1 = critically important to 5 = not very important

Figure 3 Stakeholder issues matrix.

Validation is an important part of this process (Freeman et al., 2007a). The purpose of validation is to gather together and analyze results from employee surveys, customer satisfaction polls and focus groups, feedback from industry analysts, and stakeholder dialogues with communities, NGOs, or other stakeholders. On the basis of these validation activities, the list of issues will probably require some adjustments.

Having ascertained and validated which issues are of most importance to particular stakeholders, one way to summarize the information and look for common interests is by reaggregating stakeholders and their interests back into groups in a stakeholder issues matrix (see Figure 3). A full matrix would have all the primary stakeholder groups and all of the important issues identified in the first step. One of the things this matrix can do is help identify the potential for what is sometimes called stakeholder synergy (Tantalo and Priem, 2016). This is done by finding issues that are most critical to many or perhaps even most (or all) stakeholders. These are issues that should be given priority in creating strategies and making decisions because they offer the potential to add to the value received by multiple stakeholders simultaneously. In the example in Figure 3 product improvements are critically or very important to customers, financiers, and suppliers. The example is simplified for presentation in this Element; however, a full matrix in an actual company is likely to reveal opportunities for stakeholder synergy that would not have been obvious otherwise. Another use of the matrix is to help a firm communicate with and adjust its strategies in support of particular groups of stakeholders.

5.3 Current and Potential Stakeholder Contributions

Having identified the interests of key stakeholders – what they want from the firm – it is time to identify their current and potential contributions to the value-adding activities of the firm – what the firm wants from them (Kenny, 2001). This exercise builds on the behavior analysis described in an earlier subsection; however, here stakeholder contributions extend beyond current or desired behaviors to include tangible products and services, information, and so forth.

Identifying current contributions first establishes a benchmark against which future contributions can be measured. It also establishes a greater understanding of each stakeholder and an appreciation for what they already provide for the firm. When this appreciation is shared with a stakeholder, in specific terms, it helps the stakeholder experience higher levels of value from affiliation and a greater sense of interactional justice, as described in Section 4.

For example, a firm may identify the nature, quality, and consistency of the products provided by a particular supplier. Also relevant might be the nature and quality of market information provided by that supplier, the timeliness of delivery, the generosity of credit terms provided, and whether it and its own suppliers engage in fair labor practices. This information paints a fairly comprehensive picture of the nature of the relationship between the firm and the supplier, as well as how that supplier contributes to value-creating processes within the firm.

Identifying potential contributions of a stakeholder simply asks the question: "What can this stakeholder do or provide to help the firm create more value?" Continuing with the supplier example, a growing firm might benefit greatly from a more generous time frame for credit extended by a particular stakeholder. Of course, this could also help the supplier generate more sales overall because the firm would need to buy more of its products to support its growth. This is an example of a mutually beneficial outcome. Getting the supplier to extend more credit could be a function of the extent to which previous treatment has been just and fair, and a number of other factors associated with managing for stakeholders. We will build on the notion of motivating stakeholders to contribute more to value-creating processes in both Section 6 and Section 7. At this point, the goal is merely to identify ways this might be done.

5.4 Assessment of Current Stakeholder Strategies

The transactional level of analysis is the bottom line of managing for stakeholders. It is where there is an actual interaction between a company and its stakeholders. In our experience, it is useful for a firm to identify its current stakeholder management strategies before trying to develop more productive ones (Freeman et al., 2007a). During our many years of experience with global companies we have observed at least four typical ways that companies interact with their stakeholders. We call these approaches (1) ignore stakeholders; (2) the public relations approach; (3) implicit negotiations; and (4) engagement, dialogue, and negotiation.

5.4.1 Ignore Stakeholders

Although it may sound surprising, some firms simply avoid all but necessary interactions with some of their stakeholders. When they do have to interact, as in the case of buying materials, they adopt an arms-length approach that limits their involvement with the stakeholder. It was not too long ago that this form of management was encouraged. Stakeholders outside the traditional boundaries of a firm were seen as distractions that could hurt internal efficiency. The idea was to put up buffers between a firm and its suppliers, customers, financiers, the local community, and other external stakeholders so that managers could make their internal production processes as efficient as possible. Although the environment has changed and made this management approach impractical in most situations, some firms still make this mistake in their interactions with communities, suppliers, or other stakeholders.

Ignored stakeholders can use legal, social influence, and political processes to make their voices heard if they feel as though the firm's neglect is hurting them. The key question to ask is whether any of a firm's important stakeholders are not being given the attention they deserve. Is the firm missing important information or opportunities for value creation as a result of ignoring one of their stakeholders? Is ignoring a stakeholder putting the firm at risk?

5.4.2 The Public Relations Approach

Most large firms have public relations departments or something equivalent. Many of them rely on these departments to interact with stakeholders such as communities or critics. The common thread of this approach is one-way communication. A public relations approach can apply to other stakeholders as well. For example, a firm may use press releases, social media, public events, mailings, brochures, and advertising as the predominant means to communicate with customers, suppliers, financiers, or even employees. But the key question is whether the firm is talking at stakeholders or actually listening to them too. This is an important question.

A great deal of valuable information is available to a firm that listens to all its stakeholders. Nevertheless, the most limited resource a manager has is time, and there may be stakeholders who may not typically warrant a great deal of attention because they do not hold much potential for adding to the value-creating processes of the firm and pose no real threat to the firm's current value-creating activities.

5.4.3 Implicit Negotiation

A common theme of this section is that firms should take their stakeholders' interests into account when making important decisions and devising value-creating strategies. Because such a firm has already taken stakeholder concerns into account, it can often mitigate any objections that a group or individual may have. This is a reasonable approach to managing stakeholders in some situations. However, it may not be an ideal approach because the information on which it is based is only as good as the assumptions that are being made about stakeholder concerns. A firm that has engaged in a deliberate process of identifying *and* validating stakeholder interests, as outlined previously, is in a much stronger position to make good decisions and establish value-creating strategies. Nonetheless, as we will suggest in Section 5.4.4, there are situations in which implicit negotiations may be an appropriate strategy.

5.4.4 Engagement, Dialogue, and Negotiation

In our experience, the companies that are the best at creating value for stakeholders are actively engaged with those stakeholders. They have managed to create a conversation, multiple channels of communication, and explicit dialogues with key stakeholders that are continuous. Communication processes are two-way. If managers cannot understand something, or if stakeholders cannot understand something, they make contact to sort things out. Firms that manage for stakeholders are adept at these sorts of interactions. It is through these types of communications that rich and valuable information is obtained (Harrison et al., 2010).

Firms that have this sort of relationship with stakeholders also tend to rely more on implicit contracts rather than formal written contracts. These contracts are based on informal negotiations. We have heard Robert Phillips, past president of the Society for Business Ethics, suggest that when someone says about a contract, "It is all here in black and white," what they are really talking about is the black. These are the formal statements in a contract that define terms and conditions. However, there is much more white than black in a contract. These are the implicit promises and expectations that guide most of what is done as firms and stakeholders engage in value-creating processes.

The advantages of informal negotiations are obvious. There are no restrictions on communications, and positions do not have to be taken "for the record." The expenses associated with creation and enforcement of a formal contract are avoided. Also, such tactics eliminate one of the biggest disadvantages of formal contracts – they are not conducive to creative solutions or experimentation, which can stifle innovation and thus new ways to create value for stakeholders.

When firms rely predominantly on informal negotiations with stakeholders, formal contracts can become ritualistic and virtually unnecessary (Jones et al., 2018). Although more formal proceedings may be necessary at the early stages of a relationship with a stakeholder, they are much less necessary once a relationship of trust has been established over time.

The point of this section is that firms should determine their current strategies for managing stakeholders, regardless of what they are. This information then forms a basis on which new value-creating stakeholder management strategies can be developed.

5.5 Managing Stakeholder Intelligence

This section has provided an assortment of tools for obtaining valuable information about stakeholders and relationships with them. We have called this stakeholder intelligence. One of the great challenges for all firms, especially in this "information age," is managing stakeholder intelligence effectively (Harrison and Thompson, 2014). As we wrap up this section, we will leave you with a few principles that help ensure that the stakeholder intelligence management process provides maximum benefit to the firm and its stakeholders.

1. Stakeholder intelligence management is a learning process for the firm and its stakeholders.
2. Stakeholder intelligence gathering should be ongoing instead of something that is done "once in a while."
3. Stakeholder intelligence should be recorded and organized in such a fashion that it is usable to decision makers and other firm members who interact with stakeholders.
4. Managers and other members of the firm should discuss what they have learned as a regular part of their meetings, both formal and informal. We have found that executive retreats are an excellent forum for discussing stakeholder intelligence and using it to design new value-creating strategies.

5. Some stakeholder intelligence can come from financial recording and reporting systems, but financial information should not be given more importance than other types of information in the development of strategies to create value for stakeholders.

6. Although collection and dissemination of stakeholder intelligence should be widespread across the firm, good information security procedures are still warranted.

6 Developing Value-Creating Stakeholder Strategies

A firm that engages in the techniques described in Section 5 will have a wealth of stakeholder intelligence from which to build value-creating strategies. These strategies should be based on a foundation of understanding about the direction of the firm, the business in which it is engaged, its values, and its culture. We discuss this foundation first, and then provide tools for developing value-creating stakeholder strategies. This section deals with the bottom half of Figure 2.

6.1 Mission: Business Definition, Enterprise Strategy, and Values

The starting point for establishing a mission is defining the business of the firm (Abell, 1980). Until a firm really understands what business it is in, it is difficult to determine what it does, or can or should do, for stakeholders. Typically firms begin by looking at the customers for their products and services. The question "Who is being satisfied?" deals with the markets in which a firm works. Firms may target specific types of customers (called a focus strategy) or they may have a broad approach to the market. A second question, "What is being satisfied?", deals with the specific functions provided to customers. Does the firm provide physical products, services, financial assets, or intangible assets? Finally, "How are we satisfying those needs?" provides more specificity regarding the processes the firm uses to produce the products and services that satisfy its customers. A part of the answer to this question deals with ownership. Does the firm provide a complete transfer of assets (e.g., products) to its customers, does it distribute products or services provided by other companies, does it sell rights to use assets for a defined time period, or does it simply broker deals that connect buyers and sellers (Weill et al., 2011)?

As an example of a business definition, Federal Express is engaged in shipping services that involve high-tech logistics, retail outlets, and a fleet of jets and ground vehicles for a wide variety of global consumers. They do a few other things, but this business definition covers the bulk of their value-creating activities. This is not to say that a business definition cannot or should not change, but a definition like this provides some grounding to the types of value-creating strategies a firm might pursue. Highly diversified firms may have a more complicated business definition; however, typically stakeholder strategies are developed within one of the business units of a larger firm.

In Section 1 we introduced the concept of an enterprise strategy, the purpose of the firm, or what it intends to do for its stakeholders. The question here is, "Why are we doing the things we are doing?" Mission statements often include phrases like "We promote the personal development of our employees," "We provide the highest quality products for our customers," or "We are generous in what we give back to the community." Notice that in these statements we find also some clues as to the values of the firm: personal development, quality, and generosity. Identifying, communicating, and reinforcing firm values is an important part of a firm's enterprise strategy.

In addition, an enterprise strategy should identify a firm's responsibility to society. As we mentioned previously, capitalism is allowed to function only because society allows it to function, and the modern corporation is under attack. Firms should take the initiative to determine for themselves what they intend to contribute to society. It is instructional to note that, in the research study we mentioned in the previous section, several of the interests the experts and executives identified for the stakeholders of their firms had to do with things like sustainability and giving back to society.

6.2 Building a Stakeholder Culture

Organizational culture is a system of shared beliefs, values, and assumptions that influence the way people behave in organizations. It determines how things are done. A firm's stakeholder culture is an important part of the overall culture (Jones et al., 2007). It is also based on shared beliefs, values, and assumptions, specifically about how a firm feels about and treats stakeholders. One of the most important determinants of a firm's stakeholder culture is its degree of self-regard versus regard for others. Some firms are almost purely self-regarding. These firms will do almost anything to advance their own welfare (e.g., make a profit), even if doing so violates social norms or harms stakeholders. Managers and employees in these firms will lie to stakeholders and violate implicit and formal contracts if they think they can get away with it, or if the legal and other costs will be less than the money they will make. Arms-length transactions are the norm in these types of firms because stakeholders do not tend to trust them (Bridoux and Stoelhorst, 2016). Unfortunately, firms like this do exist. As we mentioned at the beginning of this Element, Johns Manville continued to produce asbestos even after its managers understood that doing so was killing their employees. One Johns Manville manager, interviewed later, said that the company rationalized that any losses from future legal difficulties would be more than compensated for by the amount of money they were making (Gellerman, 1986).

At the other end of the spectrum are firms that are highly other-regarding. They genuinely care about their stakeholders, and they look for ways to make their lives and organizations better. These sorts of cultures are dominated by values such as trust, caring, generosity, and responsibility. They openly share resources, even information, with their stakeholders. They have a large percentage of informal (as opposed to formal) contracts with stakeholders. Firms like this exist too. We are impressed that one of the true pioneers in electric car technology, Tesla, is so interested in promoting "green" technology to help the world that they currently have a policy of not initiating patent infringement lawsuits against anyone who, in good faith, uses their technology. This is consistent with their mission to accelerate the world's use of sustainable energy. Its culture encourages employee innovation, and the company wants workers to think like they own the company. Tesla also cultivates teamwork, which minimizes conflicts. They are constantly looking for ways to create more value.

The reality is that most firms fall somewhere between Tesla and Johns Manville on the dimension of being other-regarding. We believe, and it is a premise of this Element, that a firm with a more other-regarding stakeholder culture creates more value for its stakeholders, and a large part of the responsibility for that culture lies with top management. The tools managers use to create and reinforce a culture include, among other things, their own examples of how they treat stakeholders, internal and external communications, the way they distribute rewards (including promotions), training programs, and selection of stakeholders with whom the company works. Cultures develop over a long time, and they take a long time to change.

If a manager is unhappy with the firm's stakeholder culture, we suggest that one way to begin improving it is through discussions in private and group meetings regarding what cultural characteristics may be holding back the creation of more value for stakeholders, and how to repair what is counterproductive. Plans would include determining specific actions, as well as determination of the incentives necessary to get people to start developing different beliefs, assumptions, and associated behaviors with regard to managing stakeholders.

6.3 Development of Generic Strategies for Managing Stakeholders

The stakeholder management strategies we will discuss in this section and the next are powerful tools that can help a firm create more value for stakeholders, even if they are laid on a foundation of mission and culture that is not yet stakeholder centric (Freeman et al., 2007a). In fact, some of the approaches we will describe can be used to help move the firm in more of a stakeholder-oriented direction. Before examining specific stakeholder management strategies, we will discuss some generic approaches to managing stakeholders. A generic approach can help a manager determine the amount of time and attention she or he should give a particular stakeholder in devising value-creating strategies and carrying them out.

In determining a generic stakeholder management approach, it is sometimes useful to categorize stakeholders by their strategic posture. By "strategic posture" we mean their capacity for change in order to influence the outcome of a decision. The stakeholder power analysis described in Section 5 is instrumental in determining the extent to which a stakeholder could be a strategic threat to the firm. Powerful stakeholders can wield their power in value-destroying ways if they decide to do so. The question is simply, "Which stakeholders have the most potential to stand in the way of the firm's ability to create value for stakeholders?" We might then rank them against other stakeholders based on their relative strategic threat. You will remember from Section 5 that much of the economic power a stakeholder possesses has to do with resource dependence, or the extent to which the stakeholder has what the firm needs. Political power, social influence, and position or institutionally based factors can also determine the ability of a stakeholder to stand in the way of progress toward the creation of more value, or even reduce the amount of value a firm is already creating with and for its stakeholders.

Section 5 also contains tools that are helpful in determining the cooperative potential of a stakeholder. Identification of stakeholders' behavior and their current and potential contributions helps a firm determine this potential. We can ask the question, "Which stakeholders could most help us achieve our objectives in creating more value for stakeholders?"

By analyzing the relative cooperative potential and relative strategic threat of stakeholders we have a very useful way to determine the potential of a stakeholder to affect the ways a firm creates value (Freeman et al., 2007a). Obviously we want to treat those stakeholders with a high cooperative potential and low strategic threat differently from stakeholders with low cooperative potential and high strategic threat. Figure 4 combines the

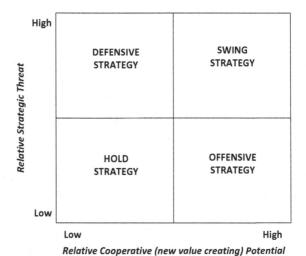

Figure 4 Stakeholder strategic postures and stakeholder management
strategies.

attributes of relative strategic threat and relative cooperative potential into
a tool that provides guidance regarding a firm's general approach to managing particular stakeholders – its generic stakeholder management strategy.

6.3.1 Offensive Stakeholder Management Strategies

Firms can be bold in devising ways to co-create value with stakeholders that
have a high relative cooperative potential and pose a low threat. We refer to this
strategy as "offensive." As there is little downside risk, virtually any reasonable
strategic program is worth a try, and any previously unrecognized opportunities
to create value should be exploited. For example, a firm may have a technology
supplier with a wealth of state-of-the-art patents that could prove very useful to
the firm in creating new value for stakeholders (high cooperative potential).
However, what the stakeholder *currently* provides the firm is widely available
from a number of sources, and it does not seem particularly interested in
influencing social opinion or political processes (low strategic threat).
Because of high cooperative potential and low threat, the firm should vigor-
ously explore ways to create new value with this supplier. The key typically is
to convince the stakeholder of the benefits of cooperation, thus aligning their
objectives with those of the firm.

Section 5 helped firms classify their current stakeholder management strategies as (1) ignoring a stakeholder; (2) using a public relations approach; (3)
implicit contracting based on known stakeholder interests; or (4) engagement,

dialogue, and negotiation. The latter approach best fits this situation. An ongoing two-way conversation based on multiple channels of communication will help encourage the release of cooperative potential in the form of joint strategies to create more value for stakeholders. Disclosure of information to the stakeholder, even important information, and sharing of other firm resources, can foster trust and reciprocity. This sort of approach assumes a friendly relationship with the stakeholder.

What if relations with this stakeholder are strained? It is possible that one of the reasons a stakeholder has a great deal of unrealized cooperative potential is because he or she is not particularly friendly with the firm and is therefore unwilling to unlock this potential through a close relationship based on engagement, dialogue, and negotiation. The stakeholder may be an employee with much untapped talent but who has bad feelings toward the firm. Or it could be a customer who buys from the firm, and could do much to promote new value creation, but does not respect or trust the firm enough to share vital information or other resources. It could also be a community government that needs the products and services of a local firm, but has a history of contracting for those things with firms outside the community. Or it could be any stakeholder that has a set of objectives that do not align with those of the firm or that does not believe in its future potential.

Adverse situations like these warrant actions in which the firm tries to change what a stakeholder believes about it. If there are no regular two-way communications between the stakeholder and the firm, at least a public relations approach can be helpful. The purpose would be to highlight positive attributes of the firm. By trying to change a stakeholder's beliefs about the firm, managers are betting on the fact that a stakeholder's behavior is a result of erroneous assumptions. In Section 5 we suggested that sometimes a firm should try to adopt the perspective of the stakeholder. In this case, we are suggesting that a firm might also educate a stakeholder about its own perspective. A firm can also use implicit negotiations – that is, including the interests of the stakeholder as decisions are made – and make sure the stakeholder knows it. This sort of strategy can engender both trust and reciprocity.

Firms in the US tobacco industry have worked very hard to change the perspective of stakeholders about who they are and what they stand for. After several high-profile legal actions that caused a great deal of negative feelings among their stakeholders and society as a whole, the tobacco companies undertook an aggressive public relations campaign, which included opening up dialogues with critics and promising more transparency than before. In some cases they even changed their point of view and began to advocate for more federal regulation and control of the industry. In so doing, they were seen as a partner with the government rather than an adversary of the people.

The tobacco firm example also illustrates another important tactic we call "changing the rules." By lobbying for new legislation that regulates the industry, a firm is in a situation of being able to influence that legislation. Any time a firm lobbies a government entity for changes in regulation it is attempting to change the rules of engagement. Similarly, a firm could attempt to alter the norms, beliefs, and customs associated with the institutional environment to which it belongs. This would be like an accounting firm attempting to influence the generally accepted accounting practices that govern all public accountants.

In situations in which the objectives of a stakeholder are different from those of the firm, two options are possible. The more difficult strategy is to try to change the stakeholder's objectives – that is, to convince the group to want some of the same things as the firm. One approach is to try to link the issue under consideration to the broader concerns of the stakeholder group. For example, consider a situation in which community leaders seem indifferent to the need for local infrastructure improvements, but the firm really needs them in order to justify a plant expansion in the area. The firm could work to convince those leaders that a plant expansion would bring many new jobs and thus reduce unemployment in the region, but it is not possible with the current infrastructure. If the firm is successful, community leaders will come around to a bigger picture of overall welfare in the community, and the firm could then unlock a great deal of new value-creating potential.

The less difficult method for dealing with conflicting objectives is to produce a strategy that is in line with the objectives of the stakeholder. This is standard operating procedure in the marketplace, or at least is should be, and can be carried over to other arenas as well. The desired end result of all these strategies is to unlock the potential for co-creation of more value with a stakeholder with much cooperative potential and little potential for damaging current value-creating activities of the firm.

6.3.2 Defensive Stakeholder Management Strategies

A "defensive" stakeholder management strategy is appropriate for stakeholders with low cooperative potential but that pose a large potential strategic threat (Freeman et al., 2007a). Often these are large stakeholders that possess a large amount of resources and are very good at influencing politics and public opinion. They may be large suppliers or large customers or a bank that provides a large amount of operating capital to the firm. Often firms consider these stakeholders friends, and the friendship should be defended because the potential harm to current value creation is high. That is, the firm should ensure that the stakeholder feels treated fairly and with integrity – any wrongs, whether real or just perceived, should be righted immediately and generously. The general question is how to prevent the degeneration of current behavior into threatening behavior.

Because the stakeholder has low cooperative potential, the firm should not spend a great deal of time exploring opportunities for new ways to co-create value. For example, a firm may be tempted to, but probably should not, spend much time exploring new value-creating strategies with a large customer that has a great deal of power but that does not possess much potential for finding new ways to create value. In terms of the broad strategies discussed in the previous section, the best approach for managing this sort of stakeholder is through public relations combined with implicit negotiations that take into account their interests. The firm definitely should not ignore stakeholders and should listen to them if they have a suggestion for a new way to create value. Sometimes a stakeholder that was previously assessed as having a low cooperative potential can switch to high potential because of a change in technology, the societal environment, or a really good but previously unexplored idea.

6.3.3 Hold Stakeholder Management Strategies

A "hold" strategy is suitable for stakeholders that are low on strategic threat and cooperative potential – they can do relatively little harm or offer only little help (Freeman et al., 2007a). This not to say that they are not important to the functioning of a firm. For example, financiers often do not possess much power relative to the firms to whom they provide financing. Furthermore, methods of financing typically are not great sources of new value creation.

The lack of threat and lack of cooperative potential means that a hold strategy is probably appropriate. Because this sort of stakeholder is unlikely to move, existing strategic programs should be sufficient. All of this is situation specific, of course, and there are exceptions to every rule. Also, it is important to note that a hold strategy is not an "ignore" strategy – a firm that manages for stakeholders does not ever ignore any of the stakeholders they depend on to create value.

6.3.4 Swing Stakeholder Management Strategies

Stakeholders that have high cooperative potential and also pose a significant strategic threat typically should be given the most attention by managers.

This kind of stakeholder requires a "swing" strategy, so called because the success of a company's new strategic initiatives could swing on whether this particular stakeholder is on board (Freeman et al., 2007a). They are powerful, and it is important to make them feel like partners in value co-creation. Consequently, this strategy involves, in essence, bringing a stakeholder into the firm and its decision-making processes, sometimes quite literally. If these stakeholders feel as though they are a "member of the family," they are much less likely to use their power to hurt the firm's value-creating processes and much more likely to use their high-potential resources and influence to work with the firm to create more value. Any of a firm's stakeholders could require a swing strategy if they pose a significant strategic threat and have high cooperative potential.

Engagement, dialogue, and negotiation are critical to eliciting cooperation from a swing stakeholder. Among the most common ways to making a swing stakeholder an even more important partner in value creation are:

1. Pursue joint ventures with them in a deliberate attempt to combine resources to create more value. These might be research and development ventures with suppliers, customers, or even competitors. Or they could take the form of marketing ventures such as joint distribution agreements or shared advertising.

2. Integrate information systems with suppliers in the supply chain so that customers, suppliers, financiers, employees, and managers have real-time information on which to base their decisions. This can make the supply chain more efficient, and sharing information engenders trust and a willingness on the part of stakeholders to also share information that can be used to create even more value.

3. Get involved in joint training programs with stakeholders. We are familiar with a US venture in upstate South Carolina that involved local manufacturers, community leaders, and educational institutions with the objective of ensuring that workers could get the training they needed to perform well at jobs needed by the manufacturers.

4. Appoint leaders of stakeholder organizations to the board of directors. This makes them a part of the team. We know a defense contractor that appoints retired high-ranking military leaders as advisors on its board of directors. This provides the firm with excellent contacts and knowledge, which is helpful in developing and selling new products to the government. This inclusion strategy also works well with customers, suppliers, retired government leaders, union leaders, and representatives from influential special-interest groups.

5. Involve customers or suppliers in design teams or product testing for new products and services. We are even familiar with a company that provides office space in their buildings for important stakeholders so they can be consulted on important matters.

This is a very short list that reflects some tried and proven methods of making partners out of potential adversaries with much untapped cooperative potential. The possibilities are endless for a firm that is willing to stretch beyond thinking about the way things are currently done to thinking about what is possible.

6.4 Value-Creating Strategies Based on Common Interests

Section 5 provided a tool for identifying issues that are of most importance to a large group of stakeholders (see Figure 3). We have also suggested in many places in this Element that firms that manage for stakeholders should receive a great deal of valuable information from their stakeholders that will help them to determine new ways to create value. In very general terms, this could include (1) possibilities for creating more value by addressing a direct stakeholder issue or an important issue for a stakeholder's stakeholder (such as the supplier of a supplier or the customer of a customer), (2) suggestions for joint programs between the firm and the stakeholder to co-create value, or (3) innovative strategies the firm itself can pursue to become more efficient or effective in what it does. These possibilities become strategic alternatives. In this section we join strategic alternatives with the stakeholder issues matrix to help firms figure out which strategies are likely to create the most value for stakeholders.

In step 1, managers in the firm screen strategic alternatives in their own minds against the most important issues found in the stakeholder issues matrix. This is an ongoing process because managers interact with stakeholders all the time. It is the essence of their job, whether the stakeholders are employees, customers, suppliers, financiers, community leaders, shareholders, or special interests (Freeman, 1984). When an idea is suggested by a stakeholder, a manager can quickly screen the idea against important stakeholder issues, as identified previously. In so doing, she or he can determine if the idea should be advanced to the next step. It is important to keep an open mind, and it is better if the manager bounces the idea off other members of the firm and other stakeholders before dismissing it.

Part of this screening process should also include an evaluation of the idea against market realities (Harrison and John, 2013). In other words, industry, social, political, technological, and economic forces should factor into an evaluation of whether an alternative is reasonable. This Element is about stakeholder management, and so our emphasis is on stakeholders, their interests, and how to engage them to produce more value. However, because we are also strategic planning consultants and trainers, we are well aware that the external environment can and should play a role in deciding on strategies, but a full explanation of this process is well beyond the scope of this Element. We should also say that stakeholders tend to be very aware of market forces, and would likely make a suggestion only after evaluating the idea against market realities in their own minds. If the idea passes the initial screening on the basis of stakeholder and market intelligence, it is recorded and flushed out for presentation to other managers when strategy discussions are taking place.

A firm does not have resources to pursue all strategic alternatives, and so it must sometimes make tough choices. One tool to assist in this process is a payoff matrix (Harrison and John, 2013). In step 2, managers list strategic alternatives along one axis of a matrix and list the most important stakeholder issues across the other axis (see Figure 5). Cash flow was included in Figure 3 as a stakeholder issue of great importance to some stakeholders. Including this issue is a de facto means of considering the costs of an alternative. But if the costs and other resources associated with pursuing

| | | *Strategic Alternatives* | | | |
	Robotics R&D Venture w/LTM, Inc.	Distribution Agreement In China	Joint Training Program	Plant Modern- ization	New Product Test System
Quality of Products	1	0	1	2	1
Working Conditions	0	0	2	2	0
Cash Flow (short term)	−1	0	−1	−2	−1
Cash Flow (long term)	1	1	1	2	0
Innovation	2	0	1	2	1
Sustainability	2	1	1	2	0
Matrix Summary	5	2	5	8	1

Most Important Issues to Stakeholders

2 = addresses issue very well, 1 = addresses issue somewhat, 0 = does not really influence issue
−1 = somewhat detracts from addressing issue, −2 = is harmful to stakeholders based on this issue

Figure 5 A payoff matrix.

a strategic alternative are not already incorporated into the matrix, they should be added.

Step 3 is the first stage of the analysis portion of the payoff matrix exercise. The first thing managers can do is look for strategic alternatives that address important issues well and are not resource intensive – that is, they don't cost much and they don't use a great deal of time or other resources. These alternatives can be removed from the matrix and placed on the "to do" stack. For example, the firm may have received a suggestion from community leaders that it would be helpful to know how many new employees the firm plans to hire in the next few years so they can do a better job at predicting the need for new schools, housing, fire stations, and hospitals, as well as the taxes they will receive to pay for community development programs. This is a low-cost suggestion that could be helpful for the community, but also shareholders, financiers, suppliers, and other stakeholders that are interested in the growth of the firm. Furthermore, it increases transparency, which might also be an important issue.

In step 4 the other strategic alternatives are evaluated based on their ability to address important issues. Firms sometimes place numbers at the intersections of an alternative and an issue, as shown in Figure 5. An even more sophisticated method weights the issues by their importance and then multiplies the ranking in the cell by the weight and sums all of the weighted scores for an alternative. We are ambivalent about this additional effort because we believe that the real value of the payoff matrix is not the numbers in the cells or even how they sum up, but rather the discussions that occur during this process. We would be just as happy with no numbers at all as long as there is some other way to summarize the results once the discussion has concluded. But the numbers do provide a sort of summary, and so typically they are included in some form during step 4.

Step 5 is when managers decide which of the strategic alternatives will be pursued and when they will be pursued. Often an alternative that ranked lower in the payoff matrix summary will be selected over one that ranked higher. This is fine. Based on our extensive experience with this method, this sort of decision tends to be driven by some other factor that was not explicitly included in the matrix. The real magic of this exercise comes from (1) explicitly including stakeholder interests in decisions about which strategies to pursue and (2) seeking win–win–win–win–win strategies that address issues of importance to most, if not all, stakeholders.

After the firm has decided which strategies it is going to pursue, it is time to establish specific objectives that the firm means to accomplish and make assignments to managers to carry them out. In other words, it is time to incorporate them into the firm's stakeholder-based control system. This sort of control system is the subject of Section 7.

7 A Stakeholder-Based Strategic Control System

What gets measured gets done. Our experience from decades of working with all types of firms suggests that this is a true statement. Measuring outcomes provides a level of accountability that does not exist otherwise, especially if a specific person is assigned responsibility for making sure that an outcome actually occurs (Harrison and John, 2013). This section is about measuring things that are important to stakeholders as they work together with the firm to create value. We begin with an explanation of how to turn stakeholder intelligence into relevant, stakeholder-based objectives. We then demonstrate how these objectives are integrated into a stakeholder-based strategic control system.

7.1 Stakeholder-Based Objectives

The first step in developing value-creating, stakeholder-based objectives is to understand fully what is important to each of the firm's primary stakeholders – their interests (Freeman, 1984). Previous sections have provided tools for obtaining this information. Some objectives are broad statements of purpose, such as, "We believe in helping our employees develop to their fullest potential" or "Our company provides the highest quality products to its customers." These statements of organizational purpose, often incorporated into a mission statement or enterprise strategy, provide a foundation upon which more specific objectives are built.

7.1.1 Characteristics of Highly Effective Objectives

In addition to broad mission-oriented objectives, specific objectives come from a detailed and in-depth analysis of stakeholder interests, as explained in Section 5. The following are characteristics of highly effective specific objectives (Harrison and John, 2013):

1. They are measurable and have a defined time frame for accomplishment.
2. They are high enough to be motivating. They move people out of their comfort zones.
3. They are not so high as to be perceived as unrealistic. Unrealistic objectives are discouraging rather than motivating.
4. They address one or hopefully more of the important stakeholder interests identified previously.

5. They are communicated and understood by those responsible for achieving them.
6. They are established through wide participation of organizational members and possibly the stakeholders themselves.
7. A specific individual is made responsible for overseeing the accomplishment of each objective.
8. They make sense in the context of what is happening in the firm and in its
   external environment.
9. They support the firm's mission and enterprise strategy, and are consistent
   with the firm's values.
10. The firm's strategies are designed to accomplish one or more of the
    objectives. If this is not the case, then perhaps the firm is missing an
    important strategy and should revisit its strategy formulation process
    (see Section 6).

If an objective is hard to measure but still important, sometimes proxies can
be used or simply executive opinions of progress made. For example, increasing employee happiness may be a hard objective to measure, but turnover may
be an appropriate proxy, along with the opinions of managers based on informal
feedback. Whenever possible, concrete measures should be used.

Of course, financial objectives associated with various strategies the firm
intends to pursue can and should be included along with other objectives.
Financial outcomes are indeed important to many of a firm's stakeholders.
A stakeholder approach includes a balance of financial and nonfinancial
objectives.

As a simplified example, assume that most of a firm's stakeholders are
interested in the quality of the firm's products, its cash flow, working conditions
for employees, and sustainability of the firms operations. Furthermore, the firm
has decided that a plant modernization has the potential to address these issues
well, except perhaps for short-term cash flow.

Because short-term cash flow is an issue of concern, the firm decides to bring
in one of its banks very early in the planning process, and endeavor to secure
a guarantee of additional working capital from that bank to ensure that cash
flow is not a problem. This objective is simply stated as, "Within 6 months
Security Bank will agree to provide us the additional working capital we need
for the plant expansion." This objective is assigned to a board member with
a background in banking, Celeste Shahin, who lays out a plan to achieve it.
As cash flow is such an important concern, an objective is set that the firm's
quick ratio will never fall below 0.5. Pat Johnson, comptroller, will monitor
this on a weekly basis. Another objective is set that the cash outlay for

modernization will be paid back through increased efficiency and volume within five years. Ingrid Martinez, who is managing the modernization process, is responsible for making this happen, and will report progress to top management quarterly.

Turning to the nonfinancial objectives, the firm sets an objective that product quality, ascertained through surveys of consumers, will increase by 10% when the modernization process is complete, which should be in two years. Hiro Zhang, marketing manager, will track this progress, and will also work with the project manager to make sure this objective is accomplished. Progress will be measured quarterly. Regarding working conditions for employees, plant manager Giovani Rosetti makes several suggestions for ways that the modernization can enhance comfort and safety in the plant. Four of these suggestions are approved and a time frame for accomplishment is established.

Finally, the modernization is intended to reduce waste by approximately 50%, thus addressing sustainability. It is decided that this is a worthwhile objective; that it should be met within two years; that Giovani will track progress quarterly; and that the results will be disclosed through press releases, social media, and other formal and informal communications to special interest groups, shareholders, employees, consumers, community leaders, and suppliers.

We realize this is an oversimplified example, but this sort of process is not at all unusual in firms that manage for stakeholders. They consider the interests of multiple stakeholders simultaneously, and thus are able to create value that might have been overlooked otherwise. In this example, employees are likely to respond with enthusiasm and cooperation during the expansion, which should help make it successful. Customers get a higher quality product, the bank gets paid on time, and stakeholders concerned about sustainability feel better about associating with the firm. This type of stakeholder synergy is the essence of managing for stakeholders.

7.1.2 Determining What a Firm Wants or Needs from Stakeholders

Thus far we have focused on objectives from the perspective of addressing stakeholder issues, or what they want or need through their interactions with a firm. However, we should mention that there is another type of objective that is just as important as objectives based on stakeholder issues. These are objectives associated with what a firm needs or wants from stakeholders (Kenny, 2001). In Section 5 we discussed stakeholders with relatively high cooperative potential. The assumption there was that not all of the cooperative potential had been realized yet, for a variety of reasons. These are stakeholders that could greatly enhance the creation of value by providing additional resources or effort beyond what they are already providing. It is reasonable for a firm to also establish objectives for gaining a higher level of cooperation, and perhaps more resources, associated with these types of stakeholders. In other words, the question is, "What does the firm need or want from the stakeholder?"

We actually slipped an example of this type of objective into the preceding scenario – the firm wanted to obtain a commitment of significant additional operating capital from one of its banks within a six-month period. We could also have added an objective dealing with employees. Given that the firm is enhancing their working environment, it could set an objective such as "employee productivity measured as total output in units divided by payroll will increase by 10% within two years." This balancing of the interests of the firm and the interests of stakeholders sets the stage for a great deal of previously untapped value-creating potential.

7.2 Using Stakeholder-Based Objectives in a Strategic Control System

The word "control" is not particularly attractive as a descriptor of human behavior. It stimulates comparisons with words like compel, force, or punish. However, strategic control is actually established to provide guidance and motivation. Importantly, it provides a means of determining whether the firm is moving in the intended direction, and helps the firm identify areas in need of attention if it is not (Lorange et al., 1986). A stakeholder-based strategic control system is portrayed in Figure 6.

7.2.1 Stakeholder-Based Control in the Context of the External Environment

Stakeholder-based control starts with the collection of intelligence. As mentioned in Section 6, this intelligence includes both stakeholder and market intelligence. No well-managed firm would think of devising strategies without considering what is going on in its industry or the social, political, technological, or economic environments in which it operates. The collection and use of this type of intelligence is beyond the scope of this Element. We mention it here simply to provide a more complete picture of the strategic control process.

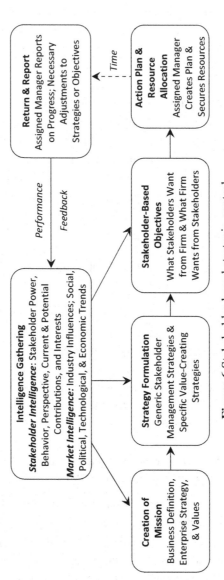

Figure 6 Stakeholder-based strategic control.

We should also say, however, that we have observed too many firms whose managers feel absolutely constrained by their industry and external environments. That is, they are still in a mindset of "adapting" to what is going on, as if the current situation is a straightjacket. The very best companies, in our opinion, consider the realities of their environments when they formulate strategies, but have a more proactive stance about dealing with them. They not only adapt to forces that can't reasonably be changed, but they also seek to change aspects of their environments to make them more favorable to the creation of additional value with and for stakeholders. We call this enacting the environment (Smircich and Stubbart, 1985). It means influencing the environment to make it more conducive to value creation. Stakeholder intelligence is a key to doing this. Stakeholders have all the information a firm needs to be innovative and successful, but the firm needs to tap it and use it.

Before leaving this important point about enacting the environment, we would like to provide some common examples. None of these will be surprising to anyone who has worked in business for a while, but they nonetheless illustrate the advantages of strategic intelligence in dealing with changes in the external environment. First, Absolute Industries faces a change in consumer tastes that is likely to make its most popular product less attractive over the next couple of years. If it has good stakeholder intelligence because of its close and trusting relationships with suppliers and customers, it will know what it can do to its product to make it competitive in the future because those stakeholders have already provided them with the information they need to know what to do. Employees have most likely also provided excellent stakeholder intelligence. Furthermore, suppliers in this situation are more likely to partner with the firm to co-create the revised product.

As another example, Absolute Industries is in an industry that has recently been targeted by special interests because of release of carbon into the atmosphere. In this case, stakeholder intelligence from suppliers, community groups, employees, regulators, and even the special interests themselves can prove very helpful in devising strategies for reducing carbon emissions *while minimizing negative impact on a whole range of stakeholders*, to include shareholders, financiers, employees, and the community. In fact, there may even be ways to reduce carbon emissions while providing more value to stakeholders as a result of efficiency improvements or first-mover advantages associated with enhancing the firm's reputation and thus making its product even more attractive to sustainability-sensitive consumers. Remember that managing for stakeholders is about finding win–win–win–win–win solutions.

As a final example, Absolute Industries has discovered (through gathering stakeholder intelligence) that its competitors are providing a package of benefits that exceeds what is currently being provided to its employees. Although its pay scales are above what competitors pay, knowledge of the difference in benefits is creating some negative feelings among employees. Fortunately, the firm regularly administers an employee survey of interests. As a result, they know what changes to benefits would appeal to most to their employees. This allows the firm to custom-tailor a new benefits program rather than simply matching what competitors are doing, which saves them money.

The new employee benefits add to costs. Where does this money come from? Should the company reduce shareholder dividends or pressure suppliers to reduce prices? Probably not. First, the company scales back its raises this year, while still keeping wages above what competitors pay. It is transparent in what it is doing and why it is doing it. It explains to employees that the modest raise this year is being accompanied with an increase in benefits and that their salaries are still above average for their industry. Second, the company experiences an increase in employee productivity because its employees are happier with their benefits and more prone to behaviors that will save the firm money elsewhere. None of this would have been possible if the firm had not been collecting stakeholder intelligence.

7.2.2 Tying Things Together

The firm gathers intelligence on the environment and from stakeholders. It has established a strong sense of direction by using this intelligence to construct a meaningful mission statement that includes a definition of the business, enterprise strategy, and values. From the intelligence the firm has gathered, and consistent with its mission, the firm formulates value-creating strategies that address the interests of its stakeholders. Also, stakeholder oriented objectives are developed based on what stakeholders need and want from the firm and what the firm needs and wants from them. A specific person is assigned to oversee the attainment of each objective. They create a plan for doing so, and the needed resources are acquired. What is left?

In the final stage of a well-designed stakeholder-based strategic control system, the assigned person returns at appropriate intervals and reports on progress made (Harrison and John, 2013). Of course, it is likely that things have come up during the interim periods that might require some adjustments to the plan. This is natural. Sometimes the environment changes, or stakeholders change, or a natural disaster occurs. The beauty of a well-designed stakeholder-based control system is that the firm is well poised to deal with uncertainty. As illustrated in Figure 6, information about firm performance measured against the objectives that were set is fed back into the intelligence system of the firm.

7.2.3 Limits to the Amount of Value Allocated to Stakeholders

One of the common criticisms of stakeholder theory is that there seem to be no limits to the amount of value firms should allocate to their stakeholders. Actually, nowhere in the stakeholder literature is there anything to suggest that unlimited value allocations to stakeholders are a good idea. In fact, there is some evidence that sometimes firms can go too far (Harrison and Bosse, 2013). One famous example is Malden Mills. Aaron Feuerstein, CEO, was so committed to his employees that when the mill burned down, he decided not only to rebuild it, but also to keep paying his workers for several months after the disaster. Financial difficulties eventually led to bankruptcy for the company. In another example, Fannie Mae continuously lowered its standards for approving home mortgages, presumably to please shareholders as well as the mortgage originators from whom it would buy mortgages (suppliers). Many homeowners ended up buying homes they couldn't really afford, resulting in a record number of foreclosures and contributing to a major financial downturn.

How does a firm know if it is allocating too much value to its stakeholders? In general, a firm can tell if it is allocating too much value to any one stakeholder if it has insufficient value to allocate to other stakeholders or for investments in future value-creating activities, such as new technology projects or research and development programs (Harrison and Bosse, 2013). In our experience, firms that allocate value most effectively are allocating just enough additional value to stakeholders so that they feel as though they are getting a better deal by working with the firm compared to other firms with which they could work. In this Element we have been referring to this phenomenon as a stakeholder's opportunity cost. As long as the total utility received from a firm is above the stakeholder's opportunity cost, and assuming that trust and respect are a part of the relationship, the benefits of reciprocity are likely to be evident.

A few general guidelines can help firms look for situations in which they are likely to under- or overallocate value to stakeholders. The criteria we are using here can be derived from the same stakeholder intelligence used to determine relative strategic threat and relative cooperative potential, as contained in Figure 4. However, in this case we are looking at stakeholder power more directly (as derived from economic, political, and social influence, and other sources), as well as strategic importance, or how much value the stakeholder actually contributes to the overall value a firm creates (Harrison and Bosse, 2013). Firms are likely to overallocate value to stakeholders who have a great deal of power, but are not strategically important. This is because their power means that managers will give them a great deal of attention even though they don't contribute much value. As we stated previously, the principle of fairness suggests that stakeholders should receive value from the firm commensurate to some degree with how much they contribute to the value-producing processes of the firm. Our suggestion is that firms should allocate just enough value to these stakeholders to limit their potential damage to the firm and ensure their continued cooperation. Managers need to be careful not to overallocate to these stakeholders.

On the other hand, firms are likely to underallocate value to stakeholders with low power and high strategic importance. Our suggestion is that managers should deliberately give these stakeholders high priority when management decisions are made. Increasing allocations of value to these types of stakeholders can unlock a great deal of cooperative potential.

Regarding the last two groups, stakeholders with low power and low strategic importance tend to be given value allocations befitting their contributions to the firm. Stakeholders with high power and high strategic importance are likely to receive a high value allocation because of their power, but this situation can be considered fair because they also contribute a great deal of value. Consequently, managers may not need to make significant adjustments to value allocations for these groups of stakeholders.

This discussion of how to know if a firm is allocating too much to particular stakeholders is a fitting conclusion to this section on stakeholder-based control because it acknowledges that there are rational boundaries to the theory presented in this Element. Stakeholder management is principles based more than anything else. Although we have described many tools companies have found useful in managing for stakeholders, the reality is that no set of tools can cover every possible interaction a firm has with its stakeholders. However, an other-regarding, stakeholder focused firm encourages manager and employee actions and decisions that are most likely to lead to the creation of more stakeholder value.

8 Advancing Stakeholder Theory

One day a friend of ours, a successful entrepreneur, was on the phone discussing a complex deal involving a Chinese bank, a European engineering company, and his own engineering consulting firm. When he finished his conversation, one of us asked him what that was all about. His immediate response was, "I am trying to make everybody happy and make money at the same time." This is exactly the point and the value added of a stakeholder approach. Stakeholder management is about making money and creating value for everyone.

8.1 Where We Are Now

We opened the first section of this Element by referring to the crises that some major corporations like Wells Fargo or Volkswagen faced because, in a variety of ways, they put short-term financial profits ahead of the welfare of one stakeholder group or another, a situation that over the long term was not sustainable. We also argued that this type of short-termism is sometimes a result of adoption of the widely held "shareholder primacy" perspective, which diverts attention away from the main function of the business firm – the creation of value for all stakeholders. Such an approach leads to many problems that not only reduce the value-creating possibilities of firms, but can also lead to ethical problems and crises that cause suffering for many stakeholders, and financial losses for the firms involved.

The stakeholder management approach we summarized and advocated for in this Element allows firms to build an enterprise strategy and stakeholder culture that benefits stakeholders now and in the long run. Firms that manage for stakeholders create better value-adding strategies because the manner in which they engage with stakeholders allows them to draw not only on the resources these stakeholders control, but also on the information, insights, experience, and energy they possess. As we mentioned in Section 2, Apple's introduction of iTunes® and the iPod® illustrated that value-creating strategies can benefit all of the key stakeholders involved – including shareholders. These are win–win–win–win–win strategies. Steve Jobs intuitively weaved together the interests of multiple stakeholders into a mutually beneficial strategy. In short, we wrote this Element to provide managers and management students with the basics of the stakeholder approach.

The stakeholder approach has for many years been associated with business ethics and the social and environmental impact of business firms. A stakeholder approach enables managers and academics to have a broader view of firm activities, including its potential social impacts, externalities, and other topics often ignored by academics focusing exclusively on markets and industries. Stakeholder theory refutes the separation thesis, which argues that business issues can be considered independently of their ethical implications. It considers business situations from their ethical, social, and economic

perspectives simultaneously, recognizing that these perspectives are insepar-
ably intertwined. If managers try to separate these perspectives, they do so at
their own peril, because such an approach does not help the firm create value
for all stakeholders, and could lead to serious problems (as numerous crises
have illustrated). A stakeholder approach not only enables managers to craft
better value-creating strategies, but also prevent the crises that often result from
dissatisfied or unfairly treated stakeholders.

We recognize that managing for stakeholders is not a silver bullet or "rules
for riches." Adopting a stakeholder-oriented management approach can be seen
as the starting point of a journey that allows firms to learn how to engage more
successfully with their stakeholders over time. In other words, firms need to
develop a strategic capability in managing stakeholders. In Sections 5, 6, and 7
we discussed a number of ways through which business firms can gather
stakeholder intelligence, use this intelligence to develop value-creating strategies, and design stakeholder-based performance measures and a control system. We cannot emphasize enough, however, that the tools provided in this
Element should be seen as starting points for the building of a capability in
managing for stakeholders and not a final destination.

8.2 Issues to Address Moving Forward

Stakeholder theory has been applied to a wide variety of disciplines, from
management and business to government and law to specialized disciplines
such as health care. The advancement of stakeholder theory might even have
achieved the status of a global movement. All this has occurred even as scholars
debate the definition of what stakeholder theory is. We are not concerned about
the precise definition of "stakeholder theory" or "stakeholder management."
Rather than a single theory, the field really contains a genre of theories with
some common elements, the most predominant of which is that a broad group
of stakeholders should be accounted for as the firm devises and carries out its
value-creating strategies. Also common across almost the entire genre is that
stakeholders should be treated well, whether this treatment is based on ethical
motivations or simply to create more value instrumentally. Of course, from our
perspective these motivations are interconnected.

To advance the theory further, rather than spending an inordinate of time in
scholarly debate about definitional issues of very little use to management
practice, we believe there are some very important topics that are worthy of
significant attention from scholars and business managers (for an extensive list,
see Freeman et al., 2010: 287–291). We list ten of them here in the form of
questions to be addressed:

1. How can firms measure performance better in multiple-stakeholder terms? What counts as performance?
2. What are best practices for managing stakeholders – practices that unlock the most value co-creation?
3. How do/should stakeholder management practices change depending on type of business (i.e., large corporate multinational enterprises, family businesses, small-to-medium enterprises, micro businesses, partnerships).
4. What are the key dimensions of firm relationships with stakeholders, and how do we observe them?
5. What are some common disruptions of each stakeholder relationship and how can the negative influence of these disruptions be minimized?
6. What are some useful categories managers consider when evaluating stakeholders, and how are those categories used to devise management strategies?
7. If we eliminate the separation thesis and accept that all business decisions have an ethical component, how does this change theory in the various functional disciplines of business?
8. What are the crossovers between/among stakeholder theory and the functional disciplines of business?
9. If we consider that capitalism is a way in which firms create value for stakeholders, what are the implications for reinterpreting the history of capitalism and its influence in the global economy?
10. How can public policies best be established that support a stakeholder approach and the creation of more value? What are the consequences of managing for stakeholders on the larger economy?

Suggested Reading

We include here a few interesting books and articles that we drew on as a foundation for this Element. We recommend them to you if you are interested in exploring stakeholder management further.

Books

Freeman, R. Edward. *Strategic management: A stakeholder approach*. Boston: Pitman, 1984 (republished in 2010 by Cambridge University Press).

Freeman, R. Edward, Harrison, Jeffrey S., & Wicks, Andrew C. *Managing for stakeholders: Survival, reputation and success*. New Haven, CT: Yale University Press, 2007.

Freeman, R. Edward, Harrison, Jeffrey S., Wicks, Andrew C., Parmar, Bidhan, & de Colle, Simone. *Stakeholder theory: The state of the art.* Cambridge: Cambridge University Press, 2010.

Friedman, Andrew L., & Miles, Samantha. *Stakeholders: Theory and practice.* Oxford: Oxford University Press, 2006.

Phillips, Robert. *Stakeholder theory and organizational ethics.* San Francisco: Berrett-Koehler, 2003.

Sachs, Sybille, & Rühli, Edwin. *Stakeholders matter: A new paradigm for strategy in society.* Cambridge: Cambridge University Press, 2011.

Articles

Here also are a few articles you might find interesting, and that also influenced our preparation of this Element. Some of them are a little more academic in their flavor, but they all have messages and implications of practical importance.

Freeman, R. Edward, Wicks, Andrew C., & Parmar, Bidhan 2004. Stakeholder theory and "the corporate objective revisited." *Organization Science*, 15 (3), 364–369.

Harrison, Jeffrey S., & Bosse, Douglas A. 2013. How much is too much? The limits to generous treatment of stakeholders. *Business Horizons*, 56(3), 313–322.

Harrison, Jeffrey S., Bosse, Douglas A., & Phillips, Robert A. 2010. Managing for stakeholders, stakeholder utility functions and competitive advantage. *Strategic Management Journal*, 31(1), 58–74.

Harrison, Jeffrey S., & St. John, Caron H. 1996. Managing and partnering with external stakeholders. *Academy of Management Executive*, 10(2), 46–60.

Jones, Thomas M. 1995. Instrumental stakeholder theory: A synthesis of ethics and economics. *Academy of Management Review*, 20(2), 404–437.

McVea, John F., & Freeman, R. Edward. 2005. A names-and-faces approach to stakeholder management: How focusing on stakeholders as individuals can bring ethics and entrepreneurial strategy together. *Journal of Management Inquiry*, 14(1), 57–69.

Phillips, Robert, Freeman, R. Edward, & Wicks, Andrew C. 2003. What stakeholder theory is not. *Business Ethics Quarterly*, 13(4), 479–502.

Strand, Robert, & Freeman, R. Edward. 2015. Scandinavian cooperative advantage: The theory and practice of stakeholder engagement in Scandinavia. *Journal of Business Ethics*, 127(1), 65–85.

Zyglidopoulos, Stelios C. 2002. The social and environmental responsibilities of multinationals: Evidence from the Brent Spar case. *Journal of Business Ethics*, 36(1–2), 141–151.

Zyglidopoulos, Stelios C. 2003. The issue life-cycle: Implications for reputation for social performance and organizational legitimacy." *Corporate Reputation Review*, 6(1), 70–81.

References

Abell, D. F. 1980. *Defining the business: The starting point of strategic planning*, Englewood Cliffs, NJ: Prentice-Hall.

Barnett, M. L. 2007. Stakeholder influence capacity and the variability of financial returns to corporate social responsibility. *Academy of Management Review*, 32, 794–816.

Barringer, B. R., & Harrison, J. S. 2000. Walking a tightrope: Creating value through interorganizational relationships. *Journal of Management*, 26, 367–403.

Bettinazzi, E. L. M., & Zollo, M. 2017. Stakeholder orientation and acquisition performance. *Strategic Management Journal*, 38, 2465–2485.

Birkinshaw, J., & Mol, M. 2006. How management innovation happens. *MIT Sloan Management Review*, 47, 81–88.

Bosse, D. A., & Coughlan, R. 2016. Stakeholder relationship bonds. *Journal of Management Studies*, 53, 1197–1222.

Bosse, D. A., & Phillips, R. A. 2016. Agency theory and bounded self-interest. *Academy of Management Review*, 41, 276–297.

Bosse, D. A., Phillips, R. A., & Harrison, J. S. 2009. Stakeholders, reciprocity, and firm performance. *Strategic Management Journal*, 30, 447–456.

Bridoux, F., & Stoelhorst, J. 2016. Stakeholder relationships and social welfare: A behavioral theory of contributions to joint value creation. *Academy of Management Review*, 41, 229–251.

Calantone, R. J., & Di Benedetto, C. A. 1988. An integrative model of the new product development process: An empirical validation. *Journal of Product Innovation Management*, 5, 201–215.

Choi, J., & Wang, H. 2009. Stakeholder relations and the persistence of corporate financial performance. *Strategic Management Journal*, 30, 895–907.

Colquitt, J. A., Conlon, D. E., Wesson, M. J., Porter, C. O., & Ng, K. Y. 2001. Justice at the millennium: A meta-analytic review of 25 years of organizational justice research. *Journal of Applied Psychology*, 86, 425.

Cording, M., Harrison, J. S., Hoskisson, R. E., & Jonsen, K. 2014. Walking the talk: A multistakeholder exploration of organizational authenticity, employee productivity, and post-merger performance. *The Academy of Management Perspectives*, 28, 38–56.

Cornell, B. & Shapiro, A. C. 1987. Corporate stakeholders and corporate finance. *Financial Management*, 16(1), 5–14.

Cropanzana, R., Bowen, D. E., & Gilliland, S. W. 2007. The management of organizational justice. *The Academy of Management Perspectives*, 21(4), 34–48.

Cummings, J. L., & Doh, J. P. 2000. Identifying who matters: Mapping key players in multiple environments. *California Management Review*, 42(2), 83–104.

Davis, J. H., Schoorman, F. D., & Donaldson, L. 1997. *Davis, Schoorman, and Donaldson reply: The distinctiveness of agency theory and stewardship theory.* New York: JSTOR.

Dimaggio, P. J., & Powell, W. W. 1983. The iron cage revisited: Institutional isomorphism and collective rationality in organizational fields. *American Sociological Review*, 48(2), 147–160.

Doh, J. P., & Guay, T. R. 2006. Corporate social responsibility, public policy, and NGO activism in Europe and the United States: An institutional-stakeholder perspective. *Journal of Management Studies*, 43, 47–73.

Dougherty, D. 1992. Interpretive barriers to successful product innovation in large firms. *Organization Science*, 3, 179–202.

Driessen, P. H., Kok, R. A., & Hillebrand, B. 2013. Mechanisms for stakeholder integration: Bringing virtual stakeholder dialogue into organizations. *Journal of Business Research*, 66, 1465–1472.

Eesley, C., & Lenox, M. J. 2006. Firm responses to secondary stakeholder action. *Strategic Management Journal*, 27, 765–781.

Fombrun, C., & Shanley, M. 1990. What's in a name? Reputation building and corporate strategy. *Academy of Management Journal*, 33(2), 233–258.

Fombrun, C. J. 1996. *Reputation: Realizing value from the corporate image.* Brighton, MA: Harvard Business School Press.

Freeman, R. E. 1984. *Strategic management: A stakeholder approach.* Boston: Pitman.

Freeman, R. E. 1994. The politics of stakeholder theory: Some future directions. *Business Ethics Quarterly*, 4, 409-421.

Freeman, R. E., & Evan, W. M. 1990. Corporate governance: A stakeholder interpretation. *Journal of Behavioral Economics*, 19, 337–359.

Freeman, R. E., & Gilbert, D. R. 1988. *Corporate strategy and the search for ethics.* Englewood Cliffs, NJ: Prentice Hall.

Freeman, R. E., Harrison, J. S., & Wicks, A. C. 2007a. *Managing for stakeholders: Survival, reputation, and success.* New Haven, CT: Yale University Press.

Freeman, R. E., Harrison, J. S., Wicks, A. C., Parmar, B. L., & De Colle, S. 2010. *Stakeholder theory: The state of the art.* Cambridge: Cambridge University Press.

Freeman, R. E., Martin, K., & Parmar, B. 2007b. Stakeholder capitalism. *Journal of Business Ethics*, 74, 303–314.

Friedman, M. 1999. *Consumer boycotts: Effecting change through the marketplace and media*. New York: Taylor & Francis.

Frooman, J. 1999. Stakeholder influence strategies. *Academy of Management Review*, 24, 191–205.

Gellerman, S. W. 1986. Why'good'managers make bad ethical choices. *Harvard Business Review*, 64, 85–90.

Graves, S. B., & Waddock, S. A. 1994. Institutional owners and corporate social performance. *Academy of Management Journal*, 37, 1034–1046.

Harrison, J. S., & Bosse, D. A. 2013. How much is too much? The limits to generous treatment of stakeholders. *Business Horizons*, 56, 313–322.

Harrison, J. S., Bosse, D. A., & Phillips, R. A. 2010. Managing for stakeholders, stakeholder utility functions, and competitive advantage. *Strategic Management Journal*, 31, 58–74.

Harrison, J. S., & St. John, C. H. 1996. Managing and partnering with external stakeholders. *The Academy of Management Executive*, 10, 46–60.

Harrison, J. S. & St. John, C. H. 2013. *Foundations in strategic management*, Boston: Cengage Learning.

Harrison, J. S., Owdom, M., Pitchford, D., & Warrant, B. 2018. *Publix Supermarkets, Inc. case study*. Richmond, VA: University of Richmond: Robins School of Business.

Harrison, J. S., & Thompson, S. 2014. *Strategic management of healthcare organizations: A stakeholder management approach*. New York: Business Expert Press.

Harrison, J. S., & Van der Laan Smith, J. 2015. Responsible accounting for stakeholders. *Journal of Management Studies*, 52, 935–960.

Harrison, J. S., & Wicks, A. C. 2013. Stakeholder theory, value, and firm performance. *Business Ethics Quarterly*, 23, 97–124.

Heminway, J. M. 2017. Shareholder wealth maximization as a function of statutes, decisional law, and organic documents. *Washington & Lee Law Review*, 74, 939.

Henisz, W. J., Dorobantu, S., & Nartey, L. J. 2014. Spinning gold: The financial returns to stakeholder engagement. *Strategic Management Journal*, 35, 1727–1748.

Hosmer, L. T. 1994. Strategic planning as if ethics mattered. *Strategic Management Journal*, 15, 17–34.

Isaacson, W. 2011. *Steve Jobs*. New York: Simon & Schuster.

Jensen, M. C. 1989. Eclipse of the public corporation. *Harvard Business Review*, 67, 61–74.

Jones, T., Harrison, J., & Felps, W. 2018. How applying instrumental stakeholder theory can provide sustainable competitive advantage. Academy of Management Review, 43, 371–391.

Jones, T. M. 1995. Instrumental stakeholder theory: A synthesis of ethics and economics. *Academy of Management Review*, 20, 404–437.

Jones, T. M., Felps, W., & Bigley, G. A. 2007. Ethical theory and stakeholder-related decisions: The role of stakeholder culture. *Academy of Management Review*, 32, 137–155.

Kenny, G. 2001. *Strategic factors: Develop and measure winning strategy.* Melbourne: President Press.

Kim, W. C., & Mauborgne, R. 1998. Procedural justice, strategic decision making, and the knowledge economy. *Strategic Management Journal*, 19, 323–338.

Lorange, P., Morton, M. S. S., & Ghoshal, S. 1986. *Strategic control systems.* Eagan, MN: West Publishing Company, College & School Division.

McVea, J. F., & Freeman, R. E. 2005. A Names-and-faces approach to stakeholder management how focusing on stakeholders as individuals can bring ethics and entrepreneurial strategy together. *Journal of Management Inquiry,* 14, 57–69.

Mitchell, R. K., Agle, B. R., & Wood, D. J. 1997. Toward a theory of stakeholder identification and salience: Defining the principle of who and what really counts. *Academy of Management Review*, 22, 853–886.

Nelson, W. R. 2001. Incorporating fairness into game theory and economics: Comment. *American Economic Review*, 91, 1180–1183.

Pastin, M. 1986. *The hard problems of management: Gaining the ethics edge.* San Francisco: Jossey-Bass.

Pfeffer, J., & Salanchik, G. R. 1978. *The external control of organizations: a resource dependence perspective.* New York: Harper & Row.

Phillips, R. 2003. *Stakeholder theory and organizational ethics.* San Francisco, CA: Berrett-Koehler.

Phillips, R., Freeman, R. E., & Wicks, A. C. 2003. What stakeholder theory is not. *Business Ethics Quarterly*, 13, 479–502.

Porter, M. E. 1980. *Competitive strategy: Techniques for analyzing industries and competitors.* New York: Free Press.

Porter, M. E. 1985. *Competitive advantage: Creating and sustaining superior performance.* New York: Free Press.

Rabin, M. 1993. Incorporating fairness into game theory and economics. *The American Economic Review*, 83(5), 1281–1302.

Retolaza, J. L., Ruiz-Roqueñi, M., & San-Jose, L. 2015. An innovative approach to stakeholder theory: Application in Spanish transnational corporations. *Revista brasileira de gestão de negócios*, 17, 1007–1020.

Rowley, T. J. 1997. Moving beyond dyadic ties: A network theory of stakeholder influences. *Academy of Management. The Academy of Management Review*, 22, 887–910.

Rumelt, R. 2011. *Good strategy/bad strategy: The difference and why it matters*, London: Profile Books.

Schrempf, J. 2012. The delimitation of corporate social responsibility: Upstream, downstream, and historic CSR. *Business & Society*, 51, 690–707.

Schrempf-Stirling, J., Bosse, D. A., & Harrison, J. S. 2013. Anticipating, preventing, and surviving secondary boycotts. *Business Horizons*, 56, 573–582.

Shane, P. B., & Spicer, B. H. 1983. Market response to environmental information produced outside the firm. *Accounting Review*, 58(3), 521–538.

Sisodia, R., Wolfe, D., & Sheth, J. N. 2007. *Firms of endearment: How world-class companies profit from passion and purpose*. Upper Saddle River, NJ: Wharton School Publishing.

Smircich, L., & Stubbart, C. 1985. Strategic management in an enacted world. *Academy of Management Review*, 10, 724–736.

Stout, L. A. 2012. *The shareholder value myth: How putting shareholders first harms investors, corporations, and the public*. San Francisco, CA: Berrett-Koehler.

Su, W., & Tsang, E. W. 2015. Product diversification and financial performance: The moderating role of secondary stakeholders. *Academy of Management Journal*, 58, 1128–1148.

Tantalo, C., & Priem, R. L. 2016. Value creation through stakeholder synergy. *Strategic Management Journal*, 37, 314–329.

Utterback, J. M., & Abernathy, W. J. 1975. A dynamic model of process and product innovation. *Omega*, 3, 639–656.

Walter, A. 2003. Relationship-specific factors influencing supplier involvement in customer new product development. *Journal of Business Research*, 56, 721–733.

Wasserman, S. & Faust, K. 1994. *Social network analysis: Methods and applications*. Cambridge: Cambridge University Press.

Weill, P., Malone, T. W., & Apel, T. G. 2011. The business models investors prefer. *MIT Sloan Management Review*, 52, 17.

Wicks, A., & Harrison, J. 2015. A practitioner critique of a conceptual paper on measuring value and performance. *Stakeholder Management & Stakeholder Responsibilities eJournal*, 4(17), 1–21.

Zyglidopoulos, S. 2002. The social and environmental responsibilities of multinationals: Evidence from the Brent Spar case. *Journal of Business Ethics*, 36(1/2), 141–151.

Acknowledgments

We are indebted to many colleagues, students, critics, and practicing business managers for helping us develop and refine the ideas contained in this Element. In particular, we gratefully acknowledge the work of Andrew Wicks, who coauthored *Managing for Stakeholders: Survival Reputation and Success*. Some of the material in Sections 5, 6, and elsewhere is based on that book. We realize we can't possibly name everyone whose work influenced this Element, but we feel especially grateful to Robert Phillips, Douglas Bosse, Tom Jones, Caron St. John, Bidhan Parmar, and Simone de Colle. The work of many of the authors who have had the most influence on our own work is found in a recommended readings list at the end of the Element.

Cambridge Elements ≡

Organization Theory

Nelson Phillips
Imperial College London

Nelson Phillips is the Abu Dhabi Chamber Professor of Strategy and Innovation at Imperial College London. His research interests include organization theory, technology strategy, innovation, and entrepreneurship, often studied from an institutional theory perspective.

Royston Greenwood
University of Alberta

Royston Greenwood is the Telus Professor of Strategic Management at the University of Alberta, a Visiting Professor at the University of Cambridge, and a Visiting Professor at the University of Edinburgh. His research interests include organizational change and professional misconduct.

Advisory Board

About the Series

Organization theory covers many different approaches to understanding organizations. Its focus is on what constitutes the how and why of organizations and organizing, bringing understanding of organizations in a holistic way. The purpose of Elements in Organization Theory is to systematize and contribute to our understanding of organizations.

Cambridge Elements ≡

Organization Theory

Elements in the Series

Printed in the United States
By Bookmasters